# Diamondola

## "A Little Diamond"

## Mildred Thompson Olson

**TEACH Services, Inc.**
P U B L I S H I N G
www.TEACHServices.com • (800) 367-1844

World rights reserved. This book or any portion thereof may not be copied or reproduced in any form or manner whatever, except as provided by law, without the written permission of the publisher, except by a reviewer who may quote brief passages in a review.

The author assumes full responsibility for the accuracy of all facts and quotations as cited in this book. The opinions expressed in this book are the author's personal views and interpretations, and do not necessarily reflect those of the publisher.

This book is provided with the understanding that the publisher is not engaged in giving spiritual, legal, medical, or other professional advice. If authoritative advice is needed, the reader should seek the counsel of a competent professional.

Copyright © 2017 Mildred Thompson Olson

Copyright © 2017 TEACH Services, Inc.

ISBN-13: 978-1-4796-0761-7 (Paperback)

ISBN-13: 978-1-4796-0762-4 (ePub)

ISBN-13: 978-1-4796-0763-1 (Mobi)

Library of Congress Control Number: 2016920888

To Diamondola who was my inspiration as a young missionary, and from whom, with the help of her diary, I was able to secure this story.

To my grandchildren and great-grandchild who love the story of Diamondola, John and Charity (Netteburg) Pitton, and Tobias Pitton

Kristin and Olen Netteburg, Hans and Heidi Olson, Jonathan and Lindsay Gardner, and Megan Ferguson.

Special Thanks to

Ronnalee Netteburg, who typed the original manuscript

Kennit Netteburg, who typeset this edition

Indra Ashod Greer, who supplied added information

Bob Merrills, who, inspired with Diamondola's story, urged me to get the book back in print.

# Contents

| | | |
|---|---|---|
| CHAPTER I | A Day to Remember | 7 |
| CHAPTER II | A Small but Precious Jewel | 10 |
| CHAPTER III | A Little Pill | 13 |
| CHAPTER IV | Autumn Preparations | 16 |
| CHAPTER V | Protestant Preachers In Town | 19 |
| CHAPTER VI | Troubles and a Blessing | 25 |
| CHAPTER VII | Joys and Sorrows | 28 |
| CHAPTER VIII | Blessings and Burdens in Brousa | 31 |
| CHAPTER IX | Early Advent Stirrings | 35 |
| CHAPTER X | More Converts | 41 |
| CHAPTER XI | Words, Wolves, and Worms | 45 |
| CHAPTER XII | Missionary Journey in Asia Minor | 48 |
| CHAPTER XIII | Educational Problems | 51 |
| CHAPTER XIV | The Second Missionary Tour | 58 |
| CHAPTER XV | A Work That Prospered at Last | 69 |
| CHAPTER XVI | Ever Learning | 75 |
| CHAPTER XVII | Diamondola Goes Through the Valley | 84 |
| CHAPTER XVIII | Work and War | 88 |
| CHAPTER XIX | Finding a Good Thing | 93 |
| CHAPTER XX | The War to End War | 96 |
| CHAPTER XXI | Farewell! Forever? | 103 |
| CHAPTER XXII | Victories for God | 109 |
| CHAPTER XXIII | Imprisoned for God | 112 |
| CHAPTER XXIV | The Second Attempt | 125 |
| CHAPTER XXV | Where He Leads | 130 |
| CHAPTER XXVI | Tasting His Goodness | 144 |
| CHAPTER XXVII | Knowing and Accepting | 151 |
| CHAPTER XXVIII | "Tabitha, Arise" | 156 |
| CHAPTER XXIX | Honey Hastens Recovery | 163 |
| CHAPTER XXX | The Trip of the Yellow Satchel | 167 |
| CHAPTER XXXI | To Love and to Cherish | 174 |

*Alexandra, Diamondola's sister, was decorated by the Queen of Greece and Prime Minister Venizelos for faithful service in a military hospital during World War I.*

## CHAPTER I
# *A Day to Remember*

*"Thou knowest not what a day may bring forth" (Prov. 27:1).*

It was March 23, 1894, in Eskishehir, Turkey. This March 23 was going to be different for the Keanides family from any previous March 23. Oh, the weather was usual for that time of year. The sun shone on the high Anatolian plateau, yet it was cold enough to leave patches of dirty snow lying on the north side of buildings and hillsides.

The Keanides family still lived in the same apartment they had lived in since Elijah and Theodora Keanides had married some fifteen years before. There were few changes in the physical appearance of the old home, but something special was always going to happen when in the middle of the week Grandmother Keanides climbed up the crude pole ladder to the little loft above the Oriental kitchen and took down the big water tub. And something special always happened when the midwife arrived and busied herself with clean sheets and soap. Yes, this March 23 was surely going to be special—a day to be remembered.

A few minutes earlier than usual Susanna and Alexandra Keanides were hurried off to school. As the two girls hurried along the main street of the Greek Quarter of the city, they were scarcely aware of the routine activity that encompassed them. Though the early morning sights, smells, and sounds of a Turkish town generally interested the Keanides sisters, they were too engrossed in their own secret to pay much attention to them this morning. They were wondering whether the new boy the midwife had promised would be given the same name as the brother who had died the year before, or whether he would be given another name. The day he had been born had been a memorable one too, for he had been the first and only boy born to Elijah and Theodora Keanides. But he had lived only three months. The girls hoped that the boy born today would not succumb to illness, as had the other brother.

Susanna and Alexandra had never spent such a long day in school. It seemed that the day would never end, but somehow time wore on and the closing bell was heard at last.

They fairly flew through the front gate, down the garden path, and up the front steps of their apartment building. Breathlessly they burst into the front door. Grandmother hurried from the living room with a cautioning finger held over her lips. Then she whispered quietly, "Don't waken your mother and tiny baby sister!"

"SISTER! Did you say sister?" inquired Susanna.

"Yes, the darlingest, littlest sister you ever saw," cooed Grandmother softly. "You can see her as soon as she wakes up. She's so delicate and—"

"No, no, thank you, Grandmother," interrupted Alexandra, her voice choking with disappointment. "The midwife lied to us. She told us it would be a boy, and now it's just another girl!" Alexandra turned on her heel and ran down the steps, with tears of disappointment in her eyes.

Susanna stared in utter disbelief as she tried to digest Grandmother's disappointing announcement. Then she turned and ran down the steps and joined Alexandra in the back garden.

"What do you think of that?" exploded Susanna as she flopped down on the white bench under the rose trellis. "If I'd known that, I'd–I'd–well, I wouldn't have come home tonight."

"Well, I'm not going home tonight!" announced Alexandra bitterly. "I don't want to see or hear anything of that delicate girl." The sun was setting. Soon the gates at either end of the wall in the Greek Quarter of the city would be closed for the night. The evening cold seemed to be threatening a fresh snowstorm. "Come," Susanna whispered as she shivered and squeezed closer to Alexandra, "let's go over and ask Uncle Stephanos if we can stay at his place tonight!"

# A Day to Remember

*Father and Mother Keanides*

"Good idea," agreed Alexandra. 'I'm half frozen already."

In a few minutes the two disappointed girls stood in front of their mother's brother's house, and raised the iron knocker that was shaped like a delicate lady's hand, and knocked. Uncle Stephanos opened the door.

"Well, well, look at the lovely early evening callers I have tonight. Come right in, girls, and settle yourselves comfortably for a spell. I have a little bedding down to do for the horses in the stable below. I just came up to throw a few more logs in the stove. Say, how's that little sister of yours? I want to go right over and see her as soon as I'm done here. You'll wait for me, won't you?"

They grunted a noncommittal reply, which Uncle Stephanos interpreted as being affirmative. Then he hustled down the back steps leading to the stable below.

## CHAPTER II
# *A Small but Precious Jewel*

*"And they shall be mine, saith the Lord of hosts,
in that day when I make up my jewels; and I will spare them, as a man
spareth his own son that serveth him" (Mal. 3:17).*

Alexandra and Susanna sat dejectedly on the carpet-covered sofa in Uncle Stephanos' comfortable living room, looking through the mica window in the door of the pot-bellied stove. It was warm and comfortable. Their stay in the garden had chilled them to the bone.

As the girls became warmer physically, their dispositions began to improve. They began to wonder how they were going to explain their wicked feelings to Uncle Stephanos. He was just too good ever to entertain such thoughts himself. He was tall and handsome, and one of the most eligible bachelors in the country. He had a Greek heart of gold and was charitable toward everyone, just as his father had been. After a while they could hear Uncle Stephanos scraping the mud from his shoes outside the kitchen door, and soon he came in.

"Well, young ladies, I'm as hungry as a bear," Uncle Stephanos began enthusiastically, "and I know your Grandmother Keanides will have a delicious supper tonight to commemorate the birth of your new sister.

I'm eager to see the baby. They say she's pretty small, but most precious things come in small packages." A shadow crossed his face. "I surely hope she makes it."

There was a long pause. The girls found themselves warming to the new sister, in spite of themselves. Suddenly they felt the urge to see her immediately. They must see her while she was still alive. They began to feel ashamed of their unreasonable attitude.

In a few moments, the girls bundled themselves again in their wraps and hurried along the dark street with Uncle Stephanos. They fairly tumbled over one another as they scrambled up the wooden stairs to the second floor of their own apartment. They knocked, but Grandma seemed unusually slow to open the heavy door. The girls walked hurriedly to Mother and planted an affectionate kiss on her cheek. Alexandra was the first to see the baby, almost lost among the large blankets.

Susanna was soon by her side, and as she bent to place her forefinger on the delicately soft and transparent skin of her tiny sister, the baby opened her eyes, stretched and yawned. Like Uncle Stephanos, they hoped nothing would snuff out her precious life.

Food never smelled or tasted so good to the two famished girls as it did to Alexandra and Susanna that evening. Dessert consisted of cinnamon pudding covered with pistachio nuts, walnuts, and chestnuts. This was always the dessert served when the first baby or a baby boy was born into the family. But the Keanides family was so happy with the new baby that they made the meal a special celebration.

It was the custom for the whole family to gather in the living room for worship on certain occasions. Every Saturday evening at sunset the family welcomed the beginning of the first day of the week by kneeling before the icon of Christ and Mary. A special worship service before the icon was also held when there was a birth or a death or an escape from a near-accident. The worship this evening was one of thanksgiving for the birth of the new baby. Father lighted the oil jar in front of the icon, and then the family repeated certain creeds, psalms, and prayers together. It was always a hallowed time when the family gathered in front of the icon. Although unspoken, lest their prayers be tainted with faithlessness, the deep concern of each heart was that the baby would live. After worship, even meticulous Grandmother neglected kitchen duties while they all filed into Mother's bedroom to decide on a name for the baby.

"Well," began Uncle Stephanos, "what shall it be?"

Grandmother pulled the covers aside to take a fond look at the little one and commented, "Most any name that would suit the girl when she becomes mature, would certainly not fit this baby now."

Father stood quietly at the head of the cradle, looking down at the tiny head protruding from under the heavy wool blanket. "I must say she is small, but she is precious. *Very precious*!" he added with emphasis. Still thinking aloud, he continued, "Small but precious like a–like a–a diamond."

"That's it, Elijah!" Mother interjected enthusiastically. "That's it! Diamondola–a little diamond."

Grandmother broke into a pleased smile as she patted the baby fondly on the cheek. "Diamondola, little diamond. That would be a lovely name."

"Yes," agreed Uncle Stephanos as he edged his way nearer the cradle, "a small but precious jewel."

## CHAPTER III
# *A Little Pill*

*"The Lord ... healeth all thy diseases" (Ps. 103:2, 3).*

Spring turned into summer and everything on and around Eskishehir was flourishing abundantly. Wheat fields were lush and green, corn was peeking through the dark earth, and fruit was forming on the boughs of the cherry, pear, apple, and peach trees. Everything seemed to be vibrant with life. Everything, that is, except Diamondola. At three months she was scarcely larger than a newborn babe. Alexandra and Susanna, who now were out of school, tended her constantly. Diamondola's food did not seem to agree with her too well, and she had a great deal of colic. She cried a lot, much to the distress of the woman who lived on the first floor.

One day the neighbor lady came for a visit. The subject naturally turned to little Diamondola, who lay on Mother's lap. Diamondola had been unusually fussy that day, and the neighbor had some good ideas about the care of fussy babies. In her hand she carried a small dark pill. This, she instructed, was to be crushed, mixed with a bit of warm milk, and poured into the throat of the colicky infant. It was guaranteed to relax the baby, and the weary mother and child would get some much-needed rest. Theodora, Diamondola's mother, was quite receptive to any advice that might help her baby get more rest and eat better. As the neighbor rose to leave, Theodora quite readily accepted the dark pill that was placed in her hand.

That afternoon Diamondola had another of her colicky spells. Now Theodora Keanides knew just what to do: she would feed the baby as much as she would take and then give her the little pill to relax her. After the feeding, the medicine was forced down Diamondola's throat in spite of her gallant struggle to resist it. Within twenty minutes Diamondola was sleeping soundly.

Mrs. Keanides went about her household tasks with a song in her heart. At last her baby had eaten well, and now seemed to be content. Just before bedtime she checked the baby. Her breathing seemed to be labored and uneven, and she didn't waken for her usual evening feeding. Mildly concerned, the family retired for the night, feeling certain that the baby was only overly tired and would awaken later in the night to be fed.

About midnight Theodora placed her hand on the baby's chest and noticed that she was barely breathing. Alarmed, she quickly got up and lighted the coal oil lamp. The baby was blue!

Elijah and Theodora quickly dressed. Carrying the babe in a blanket, they rushed through the summer night to a doctor. The doctor said the baby was still living, but that was the most he could say. Diamondola was in shock and suffering from an overdose of opium. The doctor worked feverishly to save her life.

As dawn broke over Eskishehir, Diamondola began to rally. In a few more hours the crisis had passed and the unnerved parents returned to their home carrying the limp form of Diamondola. The solemn family gathered in the living room. The baby was laid on the altar in front of the icon. Father lighted the vessel of olive oil, and prayers of thanksgiving ascended to God.

When Diamondola was five months old she was baptized into the Greek Orthodox Church. It was August, and the weather was still warm enough for the rite. Appropriate white baptismal clothes were prepared, and she was taken off to the church. Diamondola was ceremoniously dipped three times into the water of the large stone urn that stood in the middle of the church. She was baptized in the name of the Father (first dip), in the name of the Son (second dip), and in the name of the Holy Ghost (third dip). She then was dressed and taken to the front of the church below the altar. The old priest wore his long hair in a neat bun on the back of his head. On the top of the bun he wore his round, black hat, which had a flat top, with an edge that protruded about an inch around the crown. From under his long gray beard could be seen the holy vestments that the priests wore for baptismal services. The priest went into the most holy place and reappeared with the holy oil. The old priest anointed Diamondola, and she was dedicated to God. This dedication was accepted by God in a far greater sense than anyone there could possibly realize at the time.

## CHAPTER IV
## *Autumn Preparations*

*"He shall call upon me, and I will answer him: I will be with him in trouble; I will deliver him, and honour him" (Ps. 91:15).*

It was autumn in Eskishehir, and the city folks were busy preparing food for the long winter that lay ahead. During the summer Mother Keanides had boiled red tomatoes down to a thick, dark paste and stored it away in crockery jars in the cellar.

In autumn there were other chores to be done by the menfolk of the Keanides family. The Keanides were merchants, and they had to get their supplies from the port cities before the snow fell. One day Elijah Keanides announced his intention to leave for the coast with one of his brothers-in-law. Word had come that his merchandise from Europe had arrived, and he needed to bring it home. He also needed a fresh supply of Turkish products that could be found only in the larger manufacturing cities of Turkey. These merchant caravan treks were dangerous but unavoidable, and the businessmen dreaded them. The women and children had frightening memories of plundered caravans and murdered husbands and fathers.

It had been ten years this autumn since Mrs. Keanides' uncle, Paulos Gabrielides, had disappeared. He had left on a short trip to the largest city of Turkey. Goods he had ordered were waiting for him there. They had come overland by caravan. The trip would take less than a week, and since the journey seemed less hazardous than some, he decided to make it alone. Paulos rode his favorite horse and took six pack horses with him to carry supplies.

Two nights later the neighing horse was heard at the stable gate. Grandmother Gabrielides opened the gate with great excitement. But a riderless horse entered the stable. "Where is Paulos?" asked Grandmother fearfully. The horse seemed to understand and uttered a despairing neigh. She held the oil lamp high and examined the animal for some clue as to what had happened to her son. On the horse's back she found sword slashes. The cruel truth dawned on her.

How her son died, she would never know. Apparently he had been overtaken by bandits and had been killed. His horse had escaped and returned home, but the pack horses, tied together in a group as they were, had been easily captured.

Five years before, Elijah himself had had a close brush with death. After a good day's journey he and his father-in-law, Gabriel, with six other men, had stayed in a village. The next morning they left the plateau and started going up through the mountain passes. At one of these treacherous mountain precipices a group of bandits blocked the progress of the merchant caravan. Gabriel, Elijah, and the men were completely surrounded by armed bandits. The attack was so sudden and the pathway so narrow and treacherous that the party had no opportunity to escape.

They were robbed of all their possessions and arms. Then the Kurdish robbers blindfolded the men, tied them together, and prepared to shoot them. Suddenly one thrifty robber suggested that since the giaours (infidels) would soon succumb to starvation, the elements, or wild beasts, there was no need to waste precious ammunition. Caravans were infrequent, and the possibility of the merchants' escaping was unlikely.

Left alone and tied to roadside trees, the robbed men felt that sudden death by gunshot would have been more merciful. But the more religious among them began to petition God and Mary for deliverance.

It was then that Elijah Keanides remembered that in his pocket was a small penknife, a gift from his wife on their wedding day. If only he could get that knife out of his pocket, he could cut the ropes and free himself. This seemed impossible. Elijah spent hours working his hands in the ropes. Toward evening he was able to maneuver one hand enough so that he could reach his waist when he twisted in certain positions. Then hunching over, he pushed his coat upward with his hand until his breast pocket opened just enough for him to remove the penknife with his teeth. Through more maneuvering he was able to open the knife blade with his teeth as he pushed it against the corner of his breast pocket. Then, with head bent directly above his partially freed hand, he carefully opened his mouth and let the knife fall. His trembling hand at his waist almost dropped the small pearl-handled knife that represented the only hope of escape. Painfully Elijah worked the small blade on the heavy rope binding him to the tree. His hand, twisted in an awkward position, tired frequently. The friction and the tightness of the rope rubbed his wrist raw. His fellow sufferers encouraged him in the effort. His bleeding wrist complicated his task as blood trickled down his fingers, making them slippery.

After several desperate hours Elijah cut himself free from the ropes, then released a companion. It was well after sundown before the freed men were able to release the entire group. When at last all eight men were freed, they wasted no time returning from the freezing mountaintop to the village below, where they had spent the preceding night. They were on foot and penniless, but thankful that they had escaped with their lives.

Father Elijah's dread of these caravan trips to secure merchandise was justifiable, but he was a merchant and must fetch his merchandise in order to stay in business.

This time there were other men from Eskishehir ready to go with Elijah Keanides. After prayers the brave men of the merchant caravan left the gates of Eskishehir. The womenfolk and children followed the group as far as the city gates. There they gazed in solemn silence as the figures in the caravan disappeared into the morning mist. The fearful question burning in each mind this morning was, would they ever see one another again?

## CHAPTER V
# *Protestant Preachers In Town*

*"And moreover, because the preacher was wise, he still taught the people knowledge; yea, he gave good heed, and sought out, and set in order many proverbs. The preacher sought to find out acceptable words: and that which was written was upright, even words of truth" (Eccles. 12:9, 10).*

Cold winds swept down the mountain passes from snow-capped peaks. The schoolrooms buzzed with activity. Autumn preparations were over, but the merchant caravan had not returned. Each day Theodora Keanides spent more time in the living room before the icon. Each evening she stood at the city gate and scanned the western horizon for a trace of her husband and brother. But as darkness enveloped the city and the gates were closed for the night, her hopes sank and tears frequently flooded her eyes.

And then one happy afternoon the word was shouted from person to person down the busy street, "The merchant caravan is coming! Keanides and Gabrielides have returned." Theodora, with Diamondola bouncing on one hip, and the girls and Grandmother close at her heels, reached the city gate almost as soon as the caravan entered the city. She was relieved to find all the men safe and well.

It took time for the heavily laden packhorses to inch their way through the afternoon traffic, but at last they stood by the Keanides' warehouse to be unloaded. "I have a special present for you in this big box, my darling," Elijah confided as he tenderly kissed his wife. "You'll be the envy of all the women in the city."

In the living room that evening the girls opened their presents. There was also something for Grandmother and Diamondola, but the best present of all was the gift for Theodora. It was a hundred-piece setting of beautiful hand-painted Dresden china—all snowy white with raised edges and delicate flowers in little clusters.

Life moved on that winter. Many happy occasions saw the new Dresden dishes on the Keanides' table.

It had been an exceptionally hard winter, and many of the old and weak had died. Diamondola had survived, but her little pinched face seemed to grow thinner each passing day. If she could only live until summer, when she could get some fresh air and sunshine, she might improve. However, the March of her first birthday brought a snowstorm that made the old-timers shake their heads in astonishment. Nothing moved for several days.

Easter, the harbinger of spring, finally arrived. Then came summer, and happily, the summer sunshine and diet added flesh and color to little Diamondola. This sign of renewed health brought hope of her survival. Yet, another grave concern nagged at the family—at fifteen months Diamondola was not walking properly. She walked around the horsehair sofa and toddled behind Grandmother Keanides, holding onto her dark billowing skirts. But she would not walk alone.

In July, the arrival of two strangers in town interrupted the otherwise tranquil summer for the Keanides. The whole soul-shaking experience affected the lives of the family to such an extent that it became one of the most outstanding events in their history. It marked the beginning of a new era.

One summer evening Elijah Keanides arrived in the yard with two gentlemen. Susanna and Alexandra inspected them carefully from the upstairs veranda. The men were dressed in European suits of coarse wool, wore white collars with no ties, and appeared to be foreigners. Each of them carried a small black valise. Who were they? the girls wondered. And what could father want with them? Father ushered the men into the house and seated them in the living room. Then he hurried to the kitchen to talk with Mother and Grandmother.

Two curious girls tiptoed along the veranda to the kitchen end.

They flattened their bodies against the house next to the screen door and eavesdropped.

"Can we share our supper, Theodora, with these strangers? And could they sleep in the guest room for the night?" father asked in quiet tones.

"Of course, Elijah," answered his wife. "Strangers are always welcome in our house, as long as they are of good character. Are they merchants?"

"We-11-1-1, no-o," father replied hesitatingly. "They came to my shop this afternoon and I've been visiting with them—" father continued, trying to avoid a direct answer.

"Just a minute, Elijah. I think we have two eavesdroppers," and as Theodora opened the screen door to the veranda, Susanna landed at her feet. "Susanna, get up, and Alexandra, come in. I don't want you girls to eavesdrop on adult conversation! You know that! Now both of you go into the dining room and set the table with the Dresden china. We are having two extra for supper. Later we will talk about girls who disobey!"

The embarrassed girls slunk into the dining room and began the task without a word. Inquisitive and unrepentant Susanna, however, insisted upon setting the table at the kitchen end of the dining room, and hung very close to the buffet that stood beside the kitchen door. Suddenly she let a plate slip with a thud onto the white damask tablecloth. Fortunately, the pad underneath was thick, or the plate might have broken.

Alexandra looked up sharply. "Susanna, watch what you're doing or you'll break something! Aren't we in enough trouble?"

"Great Greek warriors!" exclaimed Susanna in an undertone, completely ignoring Alexandra's concern for the plate that had narrowly escaped being broken. "They-they are Protestant preachers!"

"Who are Pro-Pro-Protestant preachers?" questioned Alexandra in a subdued tone, grabbing Susanna by the shoulders and shaking her. Susanna pointed in the direction of the living room. "Honest! I just heard Father say something, and then Grandmother said, 'Protestant preachers! Elijah Keanides! How could you! How could you, a deacon of the Orthodox Church, bring Protestant preachers into your house for shelter. You can't keep them here! What will the neighbors say?'"

"O-o-o-oh, what will they say?" echoed Alexandra.

Susanna's eyes sparkled with excitement. "Imagine! Protestant preachers eating and sleeping at our house!" And then, after a brief pause, "I've just got to go in and get a better look at them. They're kind of scary, 'cause they say Protestants have pinched nerves in their brains—kind of crazy." Susanna clapped her hand over her mouth to suppress a giggle.

"It's not funny, Susanna," scolded Alexandra. "Don't you know that we aren't supposed to have anything to do with those heretics? There isn't a single Protestant in our whole town, and they have no business being here. What will the priest think of father for inviting them here? We'll have trouble when we start back to school, too. Oh, dear, I agree with Grandmother—why did Father bring those men home?" worried Alexandra.

"Oh, don't be silly," retorted the optimistic Susanna. "Listen, the children will all crowd around us, and oh-oh, won't I have fun entertaining them with stories about father's Protestant preachers!" And Susanna gave a gleeful little squeal.

"Susanna! You will tell the truth. I won't be embarrassed by your wild tales. I never know what you will do or say next!" stormed Alexandra. "I just ..."

Mother, looking grim and resigned, came out of the kitchen with Father and walked through the dining room. The girls stopped their chatter immediately and got back to setting the table. That is, Alexandra returned to her task. But Susanna? The minute both parents had their backs turned she padded softly behind them and peeked around the dining room door into the living room. She saw that the purpose of the trek was to introduce the men to Mother, who in true Eastern custom was making a magnificent attempt at being hospitable. However, the girls knew how she really felt in her heart. As for Grandmother, she didn't intend to get involved. She remained in the kitchen and sputtered about "those Protestants." Had those men been near the kitchen and understood Greek, they would certainly have left Eskishehir that very night. Grandmother's language seldom included intemperate terms, but that night she uttered some derogatory names that the shocked girls had never even heard before.

In a short time, a delicious supper was ready on the Keanides table. The men ate heartily, but the girls observed that Mother and Grandmother made no effort to share in the table talk.

That evening, while the women washed the dishes and cleaned the dining room, Father made brief calls on all the relatives and close neighbors, inviting them to assemble at the Keanides home at seven o'clock.

Out of courtesy to Elijah some folks came, but except for old Uncle Demetrius, not many were interested.

Protestant missionaries in those pioneer days traveled and lived much the same as the apostles did during the days of Paul. They were men of faith and courage, who depended upon God to lead them to the honest in heart. With only a change of clothes and their Bibles in their valises, they traveled from one city to another preaching the gospel to anyone who would listen. Their work was often hazardous and discouraging. Often they were persecuted. But everywhere they went they found some seeking truth. To them Elijah Keanides was obviously such a soul. In God's providence, these men had been led to his shop that afternoon.

The visiting ministers spent the next few months at the Keanides home. They took turns teaching their doctrines to the adults that attended. To the youth, they told many stories about the apostles and the love of Jesus. They urged their listeners to read God's Word and approach God directly in prayer through Jesus Christ. They proved from the Bible that confession of sins need be made only to Jesus and the one wronged, thus eliminating the need for the confessional work of the priests.

The preachers also explained that the saints and the virgin Mary were not ministering in heaven. The truth struck home with forceful clarity. Why pray to images and icons? That night Elijah tossed on his bed as he endeavored to come to a decision. In the morning, there was a serious consultation in the kitchen with Mother and Grandmother. Naturally, the ubiquitous eavesdropper, Susanna, was on hand to listen in on as much of the conversation as she could.

Grandmother was speaking in an undertone. "You know, Elijah, that I was opposed to those preachers. But what they say seems to come right from the Word of God." She paused as if making a decision, then continued, "Yes, I believe that they should be destroyed and burned. What is your opinion, Theodora?" Grandmother asked.

"I have to confess I hate having to do it, but there's no doubt that they should be destroyed and burned," conceded Theodora. Susanna quickly withdrew from her hiding place, and with wild terror in her eyes, burst into the bedroom that she shared with her sister. "Alexandra, get up quickly!

Grandmother, Father, and Mother are going to destroy and burn someone. I surely hope it's not the Protestant preachers!"

This startling announcement brought Alexandra from her bed like a bolt of lightning. "Susanna, you silly thing, Father would never hurt anyone! You're either dreaming or else inventing the worst story of your life! If this is one of your jokes—I'll-I'll--" Abruptly she stopped the lecture, for at that moment the most horrifying sounds emanated from the living room. It sounded as if someone were breaking the wall with a hammer; then there was a dull thud. A brief silence followed.

Susanna, followed by Alexandra, flew to the dining room and peered cautiously around the door. A bit of dust was settling under the area where the icon had stood. Then stepping through the doorway, they observed with horror the icon resting on the floor in shredded bits of canvass and splintered frame. Father had deliberately destroyed it.

Elijah then knelt beside Mother and Grandmother. They gathered up the pieces and walked down the steps to the back yard. Alexandra grabbed up Diamondola as the girls followed their elders in stunned silence.

The torn pieces of the icon were laid on the walk near the pear tree. Father struck a match to the heap, and there on that early August morning the Keanides family watched solemnly as the icon, which had previously held such a prominent place in their family worship, was reduced to ashes.

The Protestant preachers, watching from the upstairs guestroom window, witnessed the scene. That day the names of six Keanides (including Diamondola) and the name of old Uncle Demetrius were added to the books of the Protestant church.

Autumn arrived, and the Protestant preachers left for a coastal city. Their work had been met with such bitter opposition from the priests of the Armenian and Greek churches that they wondered whether their new converts would remain faithful. But they needn't have feared for the head of the Keanides family. Elijah had built his faith firmly upon the Rock. He had braved the stormy criticism of the summer, and with Jesus' help, he would bear the trials of the winter months. However, little did the small flock realize that death would claim one of their number erelong, and that excommunication would make the lives of the Keanides family almost unbearable during the coming winter.

## CHAPTER VI
# Troubles and a Blessing

*"Have pity upon me, have pity upon me, O ye my friends;
for the hand of God hath touched me" (Job 19:21).*

The hand of God had indeed touched the Keanides family. They had faithfully and sincerely obeyed the light of truth that was brought to them by the Protestant preachers. The ministers were gone now, and the family was left alone. Friends and relatives no longer spent evenings and Sundays with them. Theodora became so lonely that she cried out in her distress, "Have pity upon me, have pity upon me, O ye my friends."

But no one took pity upon the Keanides. In fact, matters became worse, as one trouble piled on top of another.

First they were snubbed, then openly ridiculed, and, most recently, they had been excommunicated. This not only ended even the casual communications but brought Elijah's retail and wholesale business almost to a standstill. The Greeks had been his best customers, and now his only customers were the Turks.

The children also had their problems. Little Diamondola was still delicate and unable to walk, though her general health had improved. Alexandra and Susanna were lonely. Protective parents kept their children from the contaminating influence of the Keanides girls. However, old friends occasionally sneaked into the back garden and enjoyed a few hours with the lively sisters.

When the school doors opened for registration that autumn, Susanna and Alexandra were not among the applicants. Elijah refused to enroll them.

"The girls will have to be satisfied to learn what they can at home this winter, unless something turns up," Elijah declared. "It simply wouldn't work for us to teach the girls one form of worship from the Bible and then have them participate in the saint worship before icons in school. We'll just trust that God will show us a way to educate them."

The girls' attitude the first morning of school reflected the feelings of the Keanides household. They sat silently, resignedly embroidering their samplers. Mother brushed an occasional tear from her eye as she swept the floor. Grandmother's face was lined with discouragement as she sat on the horsehair sofa and tried unsuccessfully to get Diamondola to walk.

Suddenly Grandmother sat bolt upright. "Look, Theodora!" she exclaimed. "Look at Diamondola—she is walking alone!"

Theodora turned abruptly to see Diamondola toddling toward her and looking intently at the floor. About two feet from her Diamondola stopped and picked up a little stump of the corn broom that had broken off Mother's. Then Diamondola bent and imitated the sweeping process with the little stump.

Theodora dropped her broom and picked up Diamondola and kissed her as tears of joy streamed down her cheeks.

"How can we doubt God's love for us? We followed Him in faith, and now He has rewarded us by giving Diamondola the strength to walk."

Susanna and Alexandra forgot their sewing for the rest of the morning as they played with Diamondola in the yard. Diamondola reveled in the attention shown her as she toddled from one sister to the other. Her accomplishment was the topic of conversation at the dinner table.

Later that day Diamondola had to share the limelight with a newcomer. During the afternoon, while Diamondola slept, a new baby was born and laid in her cradle. When Diamondola woke from her afternoon nap, she clambered down from Alexandra's bed and went into Mother's bedroom. Mother directed her to go and look in the cradle. Filled with curiosity, she toddled over to it. Her big brown eyes carefully examined the little bundle of flailing legs and arms. Gently she touched the mass of black baby hair, and with a pleased expression on her face exclaimed, "This my baby. I love baby."

And so she did. Diamondola and Despina became inseparable companions from the moment they first met.

## CHAPTER VII
# *Joys and Sorrows*

*"To every thing there is a season ... a time to weep, and a time to laugh; ... a time to get, and a time to lose" (Eccles. 3:1–6).*

During the winter following their conversion to Protestantism the Keanides family had their joys as well as their sorrows. Diamondola was walking, and baby Despina was a healthy infant. There was plenty of food in the cellar for the winter, as well as a good supply of wood for heating and cooking. True, Father's business had suffered severely since he had been boycotted, following his excommunication, but the family all felt that in time this situation would improve.

Another joy came their way when they learned of a Protestant high school in Brousa in northwestern Turkey. It had been a mad rush to get Alexandra and Susanna ready, but they arrived only two weeks after the opening of school.

Then suddenly disaster struck again. Uncle Demetrius became seriously ill. The doctors worked over him, and did all they could, but the disease proved too severe, and Uncle Demetrius passed away quietly one morning.

In the countries of the East there is no embalming. Therefore, for sanitary reasons, it is necessary that the body be buried as quickly as possible—preferably the same day. This makes death seem more severe and desperate. All arrangements must be made hurriedly, and relatives notified by word of mouth or by the tolling of the death bell.

When Uncle Demetrius died, relatives did come to the home of Elijah Keanides. But this time it was different. Demetrius had been a Protestant, and he had given no indication of recanting and rejoining the Orthodox Church before he died. Relatives and friends placed a few early spring flowers upon his dead form, but did not pay the respects usually shown the dead. The implication was clear. Demetrius had been Protestant, and they felt sure that even now his spirit was winging its way toward the burning chasm.

Elijah decided to have the funeral service in the home, since it would not be proper to have the services in the church from which Demetrius had recently been excommunicated. Since there was no Protestant pastor present to do these last honors, Elijah was obliged to perform the difficult task.

As he stood at the head of the bed, with his head bowed, tears streamed down his cheeks. Uncle Demetrius was the only man who had been his friend in the past six months. Then Elijah got the Bible, stood again at the head of the bed, and read all of 1 Thessalonians 4 to the gathering.

The wooden coffin was outside the door. But so were some messengers with bad news. When Elijah motioned for the men to bring the coffin into the living room to receive the dead man's body, a man by the door motioned for Elijah to come to him. Elijah worked his way through the crowded room to the door. "Elijah," whispered a distant relative hoarsely, "where do you intend to bury Demetrius?"

"In the family lot in the Greek cemetery, of course," replied Elijah. "Don't you have the grave opened yet? It is nearing evening and we must bury him right away."

"The priest and his committee refuse to let you bury Demetrius there!" answered the relative.

"Why not?" asked Elijah in consternation. "The Keanides family have owned that lot for years, and we have buried all of our dead there."

"But you forget, Elijah—" the relative replied, then hesitated a moment—"you folks are Protestant now, and your excommunicated dead can't lie in the same cemetery with the faithful."

Elijah was bewildered and angry. He left the house and went to see the church committee members himself. But it was useless. The day ended and it was dark. Demetrius could not be buried that day.

"I'll go and see them again in the morning," Elijah promised his wife and mother as he wearily took off his shoes and prepared to relax for a few hours before the sun would again herald another day.

In the morning matters were no different. In the afternoon things were still the same. The third day Elijah begged the Armenian Orthodox Church to allow him to bury Demetrius in an obscure corner of their cemetery. But the Armenians also refused, because Demetrius was Greek, and if the Greeks wouldn't have him, why should the Armenians risk contamination. In the afternoon of the third day Elijah went to the Moslems. But the Moslem Turks certainly didn't want to desecrate their cemetery by having an infidel buried among them.

On the morning of the fourth day Elijah Keanides was desperate. The body of Uncle Demetrius was decaying in his home. He had to get rid of it, but how? They had family worship and prayed that Jesus would show them a way. As Elijah rose from his knees an idea struck him: "I'll go to the city officials and ask them for permission to bury Demetrius in a piece of land far from the city that is not owned by anyone."

The government officials were understanding, and soon gave Elijah permission to bury Demetrius in the potter's field. Elijah secured the help of a few young men, and together they carried the coffin to the cemetery. As they passed along the street leading out of the city, men and boys spat upon the coffin and hurled taunting words at the despairing mourner—"You'd better get back in the church yourself, you infidel Elijah Keanides, or worse will happen to you."

Elijah ignored the threats, but determined to leave Eskishehir for Brousa, where his family could live near a Protestant church and a Protestant school.

## CHAPTER VIII
# Blessings and Burdens in Brousa

*"All things work together for good to them that love God" (Rom. 8:28).*

Elijah believed there were advantages in Brousa to compensate for the sacrifice of moving. The Protestant church would prove a source of spiritual encouragement for the family. The older girls could live at home and attend the American mission school. So the Keanides moved to Brousa.

Elijah opened a new business—one that was less hazardous than merchandising, though it was less lucrative. In the city of Brousa he rented a small shop and set up business as a men's tailor. In the spring of 1897 Alexandra graduated from the American High School with honors. Work for girls was scarce in the summer, so Alexandra began to sew. First she practiced her dressmaking on the family. Despina and Diamondola were dressed like twins, and their playing in the front yard became Alexandra's best advertisement. Soon ladies in the community brought their sewing to Alexandra.

Mr. Keanides earned a reputation for being an honest tailor with average ability, but tailoring did not agree with his health. After one year of sitting hunched over a pedal sewing machine in the poorly lighted and ventilated shop, he developed stomach trouble. His ailment began to keep him at home almost as many days a week as he spent in the shop.

Mother was more than busy. Besides caring for Grandmother and Father, she had Diamondola to nurse. Diamondola had always been a poor eater, and her frail body seemed especially susceptible to disease. During the fig season she developed an infection in the ankle, which in the winter penetrated to the bone. The doctor forbade her to eat fruit and insisted that she take cod-liver oil. This unpalatable substance was often refused by the child's sensitive stomach. The infection spread, and another ulcer developed behind her knee.

Theodora Keanides had many good reasons for being discouraged, but this plucky little Greek woman clung to the words of Paul to the Roman believers. She believed that someday she would see how all these things had worked together for good, for she truly loved the Lord.

Every day Mother carried Diamondola to the doctor to have her ulcers treated, but each day they seemed to become worse. Theodora tried some of her own treatments. When the summer of 1898 arrived, she began letting Diamondola stay out in the sunshine, and gave her fruit and plenty of water. Within a few weeks the ulcers began to heal.

The same summer that brought renewed health to Diamondola and respite from pain to Father, brought the end for Grandmother. One day she slipped quietly to her rest.

After Grandmother was buried, Theodora decided to take up a line of work at home that would supplement the family income. Since Brousa was a city well known for its silk industry, she purchased a loom and began to weave for merchants by contract. This proved to be satisfactory. Susanna helped her when she could, and four-and-a-half-year-old Diamondola wound the bobbins.

Susanna graduated from the American High School in the spring of 1899, and another loom was purchased and set up for her. With the three women working at home, the financial burden lightened, and Father was not so worried about money matters as he had been. It appeared certain that he would never regain his robust health, and he accepted his life of semi-invalidism with resignation. He only worked when he could, and cheered the others when he was forced back to his bed. The combined earnings were sufficient to keep the family supplied with their daily needs.

About this time a young barber who lived across the valley began to come to "visit Father." But the young man's gaze seemed to linger upon Susanna's vanishing form like sunshine on distant mountaintops.

As the visits continued, Susanna often stayed in the room with Father and Stavro, but Diamondola observed with envy that the rest of the family was not allowed the same privilege.

As Stavro's intentions became plainer, Father cautioned Susanna about her friendship with an unbeliever. But by this time Susanna had become too involved to pay him much heed.

"Father," she reasoned, "Stavro and I love each other, and we'll not make an issue of religion. I'll always be a Protestant in my heart. I'm nineteen now, and should marry, if I'm ever going to. Stavro is honest and clean, and makes a fair living. We will be happy, you'll see," she insisted.

"My dear Susanna," Elijah cautioned, "I know that you feel you will never find a young man among the Protestants. Be that as it may, the Bible injunction is, 'Be ye not unequally yoked,' and you will be unequally yoked." But Susanna had her way.

The day of the wedding arrived. Father and Mother were solemn as they realized that the happy family circle would now be broken. But hardest of all was the thought that in Susanna's home there would be no family worship circle, only broken links—an unequal union. Stavro, the handsome groom, was a relative of the Greek Orthodox bishop of Salonika (Thessalonica), Greece. He was a member of that church, and Susanna belonged to the Protestant church, so the wedding could not be held in either church. This fact caused the Keanides grim anxiety on the day that should have been the happiest in Susanna's life.

There was another lesser reason for concern. After Susanna established her own home, her monthly silk cloth money would be eliminated from the family's income. Father had not been feeling well, and would be unable to work for some time. The bills would mount faster than the income, and Mother and Alexandra would be left alone to struggle with this financial problem. But this problem would somehow be solved.

When autumn came the Keanides held a family council, after which Mother and Alexandra made out a regular program the little girls were expected to follow rigidly. In the autumn of 1899 Diamondola and Despina had been enrolled in the Protestant kindergarten school in Brousa. Because of a massacre of Armenians this school had been transformed into an orphanage, so that when school had opened in the fall of 1900 Diamondola and Despina had had to attend the Greek Orthodox school. Here they had undergone so much persecution that Elijah resolved not to send them to school again. It was decided then that Alexandra was to teach them arithmetic, reading, and English, and that father was to teach them Bible, history, and geography.

This arrangement proved most satisfactory, and the girls made excellent progress. During the next few years the home was the only school Diamondola and Despina knew as they followed the study-work-play program outlined by Alexandra.

In the summer of 1902 Diamondola began having ulcerated sores again. One developed in the groin of her leg, which defied any method of treatment and continued to grow in circumference and depth. At last the sore so debilitated Diamondola that she had to be confined to her bed. In March, 1903, the doctor decided that the ulcer must be operated on. After much persuasion Diamondola agreed to be placed on the dining room table and accept the injection the doctor promised would alleviate the pain of lancing the ulcer. She lay trembling on the table, fists clenched, teeth chattering, and praying. The doctor raised the needle. A twinge of pain accompanied the emptying of the syringe. This pain was followed swiftly by a terrible burning sensation that caused Diamondola to leap from the table and tear madly about the room.

Fortunately, after the initial shock of the injection the pain subsided, and Diamondola began to regain her composure. When reason returned, Diamondola crept meekly back onto the table. She was completely exhausted, for it had been weeks since she had engaged in any type of activity.

"I'm not going to cry," she determined as she gritted her teeth. When the doctor started to cut deeply into the sore she never flinched. She even flashed a smile of courage in her mother's direction and said bravely, "Look, Mother, it's not hurting. I'm not crying. It's not hurting." She continued to be courageous even when she felt her stomach twist into knots as the doctor cut deeper and deeper. Then the room seemed to spin, and voices faded out, but still she mumbled on bravely, "It's-it's not hurting, Mother." However, the beads of perspiration on her pallid forehead belied the words of courage that escaped her pinched lips.

The doctor worked on. He removed a large white lump from the center of the infection. The wound was then cleansed and bandaged, and limp from exhaustion, she was lifted from the dining room table and placed in her own bed. Within eight weeks the wound was healed, but three scars remained. By summer she was completely well.

*CHAPTER IX*
# Early Advent Stirrings

"And it shall come to pass in that day, that the Lord shall set his hand again the second time to recover the remnant of his people, which shall be left, from Assyria, and from Egypt, and from Pathros, and from Cush, and from Elam, and from Shinar, and from Hamath, and from the islands of the sea" (Isa. 11:11).

In the late 1880s the time for the fulfillment of Isaiah 11:11 arrived. The truth of the gospel must be brought the second time to the lands of the Middle East.[1] Five years before Diamondola Keanides was born, the Seventh-day Adventist message was introduced into Asia Minor by Theodore Anthony, a Greek shoemaker who had lived in America. He returned to Constantinople (Istanbul) to teach Adventism, which he had accepted in California. His occupation was preaching, but he had to support himself by cobbling. His first convert was Zadour G. Baharian, the son of his landlord. This young Armenian went immediately to Basel, Switzerland, to

---

1   The Seventh-day Adventist work in the Middle East was first begun in Egypt about 1880 by Dr. Hetbert Ribron, who had been baptized by J. N. Andrews. He settled in Alexandria, Egypt, where he labored and won two Italians. However, the three were killed in 1882 in a riot connected with the Arabi-Pasha's revolt. Work did not begin again in Egypt until 1899—Adventist work in Syria, Palestine, and Lebanon was started about 1900, and in Persia about 1911.

prepare himself for the ministry in the Adventist Church. After two years of study Baharian returned to Turkey. In 1892 he entered upon his arduous and fruitful labors, and soon earned the title of the "second Paul."

Baharian's mission field was approximately the same territory covered by the apostle Paul—Asia Minor, or Turkey. Burning with zeal for Christ, and blessed with exhaustless energy and dauntless courage, Baharian journeyed by foot or on horseback through Turkey, preaching the gospel. He was often imprisoned, beaten, stoned, and surrounded by furious mobs. He usually traveled alone, and suffered alone. Yet he was never really alone. Jesus was his constant companion.

In the late fall of 1903 Baharian arrived in Brousa, and, as was his custom, he went into the market place and talked to whoever would listen to him in an endeavor to arouse an interest in his message. Usually someone was impressed to invite Baharian to his home, where he could hold cottage meetings for the interested ones. Elijah Keanides was in the marketplace the day Baharian arrived, but he hesitated to invite Baharian to his home as he recalled, with a smile, Theodora's reaction to the Protestant preachers several years before. But Elijah did go to the cottage meetings of the Sabbatarian. The girls attended also, occasionally, but Theodora refused to be interested.

Baharian's preaching was direct and clear, appealing to the intellect as well as the heart. Elijah accepted his message. When he announced to Theodora that he was going to become a Seventh-day Adventist, she exclaimed in ridicule and anger, "Elijah, you aren't! You wouldn't! What will people think of you—a man who is always changing his mind. First you were Greek Orthodox, then you changed to Protestant, now you want to be baptized a Sabbatarian and join their small group! I'm sure no one else in the whole city of Brousa will be a Sabbatarian with you!"

"Yes," answered Elijah calmly and patiently, "there will be two others—maybe more—baptized with me. We will make a very small nucleus, but ..."

"And," interrupted Theodora, shaken to tears, "you will be one of the few in Brousa to be a Seventh-day Advent. That's no distinction. Already our children are suffering because of your attending Baharian's meetings. Haven't they endured enough by being Protestants? Now the children on the street taunt them by calling them Jews! Must we always be outcasts—infidels to an intolerant society, Protestant pigs to the Orthodox? We have been robbed by bandits, reduced from house owners to tenants, from respectable citizens to nobodies weaving silk. Through all this I have

*Elder Z.G. Baharian, who brought the Sabbath truth to the Keanides family.*

not complained. But this! This is just too much. I can bear it no longer." Theodora dropped to a chair, buried her head in her hands and wept.

Elijah was touched. In all of his years with Theodora he had never seen her unreasonable. She never complained. Her cheerful, courageous spirit was often the source of his strength. She came from a well-bred, comfortably situated family. When she married him it looked as if she would never lack anything. But fate had dealt cruelly with them, and he could not blame Theodora for the way she felt.

Elijah tried patiently and earnestly to explain to Theodora why he had accepted this new religion. But Theodora, now calm and collected, did not understand his faith though she understood his feelings. She made it clear that she had no intention of embracing this new doctrine.

From that day on Elijah and Theodora led separate religious lives. She entreated her daughters not to join their father's faith, but she did not positively forbid them to attend the meetings with him. Theodora wanted no religious discussions in the home, but Elijah found it impossible to comply with this request. After Baharian left Brousa, visitors and neighbors often came to study the Bible with Elijah, so that he became a missionary in his own home and community.

In the spring of 1904 Alexandra, along with a number of neighbors and friends, accepted her father's faith and joined the church through baptism. Elijah successfully nourished the seeds of truth that Baharian had planted. Now there was a fair-sized group of Adventists meeting each week, and when a church company was organized in Brousa, Elijah was made local elder.

One day in the summer of 1904 Elijah received a letter from Brother Baharian, written from the Tarsus district. It said he was imprisoned for the truth's sake. Other Christian organizations had become jealous of his zeal and the progress of his work, and had falsely accused him to the government. But Baharian loved not his life unto death, and like Paul from his prison in Rome, Baharian sent out his letters as faithfully as ever to the church elders and scattered members throughout Turkey. The prison authorities took note of the frequency with which he wrote to some persons, and the addresses were placed on the dangerous-suspects file. Surely, the authorities thought, if Baharian is a dangerous political agitator, his accomplices must be little better. So Baharian's letters were the scent the wolves needed to send them on the trail of the other sheep.

One late afternoon Theodora and the three girls were returning from a walk. As they turned down the lane that led to their home they noticed that their door had been wrenched from its hinges. Fear gripped their hearts as they hurried homeward. The place looked as if it had been struck by a cyclone. The contents of the drawers and trunks had been dumped in the middle of the floors. Papers, books, and winter clothing lay scattered everywhere. Theodora was the first to notice that every letter had been taken, and her suspicions were immediately aroused. Closer investigation showed that Baharian's letters, Father's Sabbath School lessons, and all Adventist literature were gone.

Diamondola and Despina were sent to bring Elijah from his shop on the double, but when they got there they found the door barred. Neighboring shopkeepers informed the little girls that the police had just taken their father off to prison. The men were sympathetic, for they all liked Elijah Keanides. They assured the little girls that there had been some misunderstanding, and that Elijah would be released in a few days, when he was proved innocent.

The little girls bore the startling news home to their dazed mother. She knew that Elijah had acquired a strange religious quirk, but she was sure there was no citizen more loyal to the Ottoman Empire than Elijah Keanides. Theodora took food and blankets to the prison for Elijah, but was refused admission. With a heavy heart she turned her faltering steps homeward. This was worse than she had anticipated. Elijah, her husband, had been thrown in with the worst of the prisoners. He had to sleep on a bare, dirty floor in a dimly lighted and poorly ventilated room.

That night Alexandra gathered the little girls and Mother together and prayed. Her faith during the hours of this trial left a lasting impression upon the other three kneeling with her.

Upon investigation, it came out that Elijah had been imprisoned because of his association with Baharian and the Adventists. During the next few days Theodora visited the prison frequently, but was not permitted to enter. Those were anxious days for the Keanides family. Often Diamondola awoke at night, restless and tearful. At such times, she remembered that her father was sleeping on the hard prison floor, and she crawled out of bed and lay down on the bare floor, feeling that the least she could do was to suffer with her dear father.

Two weeks after his arrest Elijah was suddenly released. After he had had a good warm bath, a shave, and a haircut, the family gathered around him to hear his story.

The story was simple. The government authorities had found nothing worthy of imprisonment in any of Baharian's letters. The officers had reached this conclusion within a few hours after they read his letters, which were written in Turkish. But the English literature had had to be translated by a friend of Father's, and it had taken two weeks to get all the translating done. Fortunately, this friend had not understood, or perhaps had not read, the footnote in the Sabbath School lesson on Revelation 9, where Mohammedanism was likened to a baneful smoke.

It should be said, to the credit of the Moslem government officials in Turkey, that the evidence brought against the Adventists in Turkey, who had been falsely accused of disloyalty by other Christian societies, was weighed impartially, and the Adventists were found not guilty.

It was a happy family that knelt that night in the family prayer circle. This time the tears that were shed were tears of joy.

*CHAPTER X*
# More Converts

*"And believers were the more added to the Lord" (Acts 5:14).*

After Elijah's prison experience, Diamondola and Despina were more conscious than ever of the religious discussions that often took place in their home between Mother's preacher and their father. They continued to go to church on Sundays with Mother, but now they often attended Father's church services as well. Mother did not object to the Adventists holding some of their services in her home, but she absented herself from the room on such occasions.

After his release from prison, Baharian was joined in his ministry by several young men who also became itinerant pastors. During their brief stays, these ministers studied long hours with the church members and interested inquirers. Diamondola and Despina joined these study groups with genuine enthusiasm. Before long they were convinced that Adventism was biblical and that they must become Adventists.

During the winter of 1905–1906, Diamondola and Despina began to attend Sabbath services regularly with Father. The first Sabbath they kept they came home and discovered that while they were gone Mother had fainted and some neighbor women had come and helped her. The next day, Sunday, Mother went to church alone. All week long she felt disconsolate and deserted. The next Sabbath Diamondola and Despina again went off to church with Father. When they returned home they again found Mother faint and lying on the sofa. During the following week Father took Mother to the doctor, but he could find nothing seriously wrong with her. She was simply disturbed emotionally. It became apparent that Mother was fighting against her conscience.

That week Diamondola and Despina went through a difficult mental struggle. They knew that their mother's illness was caused by their going to church and were afraid that if they continued to go to the Adventist church their mother might die. If this happened, they felt that they would be responsible. Yet, they knew that the Bible says, "He that loveth father or mother more than me is not worthy of me," and, "Take up thy cross and follow me." They resolved to follow Jesus. That week they made Mother's health the main subject of their prayers. The next Sabbath they went to church as usual, but when they returned home Mother was well. Never again did she have sick spells on Sabbath.

Perhaps it would have been easier for Mother to accept the fact that Diamondola and Despina had become Adventists had Alexandra been there that winter to help smooth over the difficulties, but Alexandra was not at home.

In the summer of 1903 Dr. A. W. George had come from America and had set up treatment rooms in Constantinople. He was the first Adventist missionary sent to Turkey. He needed a nurse to help him, and Alexandra was asked to join him in Constantinople, the capital, in the fall of 1904. Mother was reluctant to see her eldest daughter leave home, but Father was eager to see his children enter the Lord's work in one capacity or another.

After Alexandra left home Bible studies and school lessons kept the active minds of Diamondola and Despina occupied during the week, but on Sabbaths and Sundays they especially missed their sister.

To overcome their loneliness, the girls began to correspond with Alexandra, who was overjoyed to learn of her sisters' spiritual progress. She was thrilled to learn of the growth of the little church group meeting in Brousa during the spring and summer of 1906.

While Alexandra was in Constantinople, Dr. George contracted a terminal illness and returned to the United States to live out his last days. Because there was no doctor to run the Constantinople clinic, it was temporarily closed. But the mission, having seen the value of the medical missionary work, decided to send Alexandra to England, where she could learn midwifery, in preparation for the day when the clinic would be reopened.

From England, Alexandra wrote to her family stories of Adventists in other parts of the world. How wonderful it seemed to them to be a part of this large world family. However, Mother did not share their joy, and it hurt the girls to know that Mother showed no desire to join the Adventist family.

Though they had accepted Adventism, Diamondola and Despina had not yet been baptized. One night, however, Diamondola had a dream that led her to decide to request baptism. In her dream, she was standing with Despina and her father by the open window, looking skyward. They were singing a song about the second coming of Jesus while they waited for the white cloud bearing Him to appear.

After this dream Diamondola and Despina decided to be baptized as soon as possible. Father agreed, and wrote to the mission of their desire to be baptized right away.

But the itinerant pastors had many such requests, and they were unable to come to Brousa before winter set in. However, when the pastor did arrive, even though it was winter, the girls decided to be baptized that night. Theodora objected to this. Not only did she oppose her daughters' joining the church, but she was certain that they would die of pneumonia.

The baptism was conducted in secret because of the strong religious prejudice of the community. At two o'clock in the morning the four candidates, Father, Dikran (a young convert from one of the villages), and the pastor stealthily made their way to a suitable place on the Govdere River.

Dikran walked down to the river and chopped a hole through the ice large enough for the immersion of a candidate. The minister took his place in the icy depths of the river, and one by one he silently baptized the candidates. No song was sung; there were only whispered congratulations, a welcoming hand of fellowship, and joyous but quiet tears. The minister offered a prayer on the riverbank, dedicating these new members to the service of God.

Wrapped in blankets, the group hurried home. Mother had the pot-bellied stove red hot, and on the top bubbled a kettle of delicious onion-potato soup. Everyone gathered around the cheery fire while they ate the hot soup. As they ate, they spoke of the blessings that had been theirs, God's miracles in behalf of other Turkish Adventists, and of the work yet to be done for God in Turkey. Then they knelt around the stove to dedicate themselves to the finishing of God's work, and retired to rest.

As Diamondola snuggled under her heavy quilt she curled up into a ball and contemplated the glorious experience that was hers. Sleep would not come, for a strange, an almost holy, feeling possessed her. Just as twelve-year-old Jesus felt that He must be about His Father's business, so twelve-year-old Diamondola felt that she must be about her Father's business. She did not try to excuse herself from service by pleading with God, 'I'm only a child—a weak, stunted girl." Kneeling in bed, with head bowed on her pillow, she prayed, "Here am I, Lord; send me. On the banks of the river Govdere and by the warm iron stove I dedicated my life to Thee, and here again in bed, Lord, I dedicate my life in service to Thee, and I mean it. No matter when or where, I hope I will never question. I am Your Diamondola. Help me win other gems for Thy kingdom. Amen."

Little did Diamondola realize that in less than a year God would test her on this promise.

## CHAPTER XI
# Words, Wolves, and Worms

*"For I know this, that after my departing shall grievous wolves enter in among you, not sparing the flock" (Acts 20:29).*

Despina and Diamondola were relieved and happy—they were now baptized Seventh-day Adventists. The winter of 1906 and 1907 found Diamondola and Despina working at the looms with Mother. On a stool beside them lay their list of English vocabulary words. Though they had to work at the looms, as did many of the middle-class girls in Brousa, they pursued their education by practicing their lessons in conversational English. Each evening they got out the *Little Friend*, sent to them by the new missionary, Pastor C. M. AcMoody, in Constantinople, and studied the stories until they found ten words they did not know. They would write these words on a piece of paper, and then look up their Greek and Turkish equivalents. The next day they would practice the new words until they became part of their English vocabulary.

That spring of 1907 handwritten Bible lessons teaching the importance of keeping certain Jewish feasts came to them from Egypt. The lessons attacked the leaders of the Adventist Church and Sister White, in particular. The church members of Brousa looked over the material and discerned the heresies in it. One Sabbath morning the church group in Brousa was visited by two of these false teachers, Tatarian, and his friend, Ouzounian. Elijah, on account of illness, was not present to stop them from presenting their false teachings to the group. After insinuating their heresy into the Sabbath school lesson during class discussion, they attempted to take over the preaching service. The church members were disturbed. No one wished to hear their heresies. But the false teachers were insistent in their demands to be heard. Diamondola looked from one adult member to another, waiting for one of them to put a stop to the proceedings. They all seemed upset, but no one seemed to know just how to ask the false teachers to be quiet. Silently she breathed a prayer to God. She knew it was not His will that wolves should come in among them and try to unsettle their faith. Suddenly she was moved with righteous indignation to say: "Gentlemen, you are bringing in a strange doctrine to which we Adventists do not agree. My father is the church elder, and if he were here today, he would not allow you to speak. I am his daughter, and his representative, and I will not allow you to speak here, either. If you have a message to give, you may rent a place and preach there. People will be free to come and hear you in your own place, and in your own place you will be free to speak. But this is God's place of worship, and we do not want to hear any more of your heresies."

Immediately the other church members joined Diamondola in refusing to hear the false teachers, who then got up and left, muttering angrily. The church rejoiced that they could continue in peace with their Sabbath service. No one from the Brousa group ever joined this Jewish-feasts offshoot.

That spring Diamondola and Despina determined to help Mother lift the financial burden from their patient, never-complaining father. Elijah's health had been quite poor that winter and he had not been able to work in his tailor shop. Alexandra, training in England, was not able to help them, either. Susanna and Stavro had their own financial problems. Diamondola and Despina decided that they were the only ones who could earn the cash needed. Diamondola came up with a master plan. They would raise silkworms! Many people in Brousa raised silkworms. "But," objected Mother, "don't you know silkworms are difficult to raise, unless you really know how?"

"Oh," answered Diamondola, "I've already thought of that. One of our neighbors raises them, and I'll learn from her."

So Diamondola persuaded her parents to buy some silkworm eggs, which she put on some mulberry leaves and set on a tray in the corner of her and Despina's bedroom. The eggs eventually hatched into larvae. In return for mulberry leaves and for information on how to raise silkworms, the girls agreed to pick leaves for the neighbor lady's silkworms.

They were given a dust-covered tree by the side of the road from which to gather leaves to feed their own silkworms, but they were the best they could find. The leaves of this tree were spotted with rusty specks, caused by hail and rain. The silkworm is a fastidious creature that requires dry, spotlessly clean leaves to feed on. The girls realized that these leaves were not the best for their silkworms, but they had no alternative but to use them, because the people in Brousa who raised silkworms and had mulberry trees needed the leaves for their own worms. In spite of this the worms thrived. When the time came for the caterpillars to begin weaving their cocoons, they were the finest looking silkworms in all of Brousa, and the silk they produced was sold for the highest price. The neighbors wondered at the girls' good fortune, but the girls knew that it was God who had blessed their efforts:

After paying tithe on their earnings, and giving generous offerings, they turned the rest of the money over to Mother for the family's use. Mother very wisely used the money to replace the girls' outgrown and worn-out winter clothing. Diamondola was to need these clothes for the next task that lay ahead of her.

*CHAPTER XII*
# Missionary Journey in Asia Minor

*"First, I thank my God through Jesus Christ for you all ... I make mention of you always in my prayers; making request, if by any means now at length I might have a prosperous journey by the will of God to come unto you"*
*(Rom. 1:8–10).*

In the summer of 1907, C. M. AcMoody was sent by the mission to hold a series of meetings with the Adventist believers in Turkey, in order to refute the doctrines of the feast-keeping offshoot and gather those who had been misled back to the fold. Tatarian and Ouzounian had traveled throughout the country disseminating their peculiar doctrines among the new Adventist companies.

Brousa was Elder AcMoody's first stop. He soon realized that he faced a problem of communication. Having arrived from America only that spring, he did not speak the language. Alexandra, who had been Dr. George's translator, was now in England, and Elder AcMoody had not been able as yet to find someone to translate for him. He was therefore glad to find that Diamondola and Despina understood English. It was surprising how much English they had learned at home through their grammar book, the little Greek English dictionary, the first reader, and the *Little Friend*.

To the surprise of everyone, Diamondola found that not only could she understand Elder AcMoody's message but that she could also translate it with fluency into Greek or Turkish. It seemed evident that God had prepared her for such a time as this. During the previous five years, when the sisters had not been able to afford formal education, they had used their time at the loom and their leisure hours in the home, practicing and studying English until they understood it well, especially Diamondola.

After closing his meetings at Brousa, Elder AcMoody needed to visit the other churches scattered throughout Asia Minor and reestablish their faith in the doctrines of the church. He therefore asked the Keanides to allow Diamondola to accompany him on his itinerary as his translator. The national Adventist ministers in Turkey at this time were Armenians, and because of recent Armenian uprisings, all Armenians were confined by government order to their home towns and their environs. Few of them understood English very well, and therefore could not have served as translators even if they had been able to travel. Diamondola was of Greek background, and since the Greeks had not participated in the recent uprisings, she had unique qualifications to meet the need of the hour.

The Keanides family knew only too well that the trip would be arduous at best for their naturally frail child. The question that occurred to them as they prayed about the problem was whether she would live through the missionary journey to see their faces again. Finally, the family agreed that Diamondola had perhaps been brought into this kingdom "for such a time as this." Even Theodora, though not a member of the church, submitted to what she accepted as the will of God.

So, it was that thirteen-year-old Diamondola entered upon her first missionary journey. Eagerly she packed her few new clothes purchased with the silkworm money, and waved a tearful good-by to her parents and her companion, Despina.

Elder AcMoody and Diamondola spent several months traversing the land of Turkey, visiting the Adventist companies and individual members. By the grace of God, they were able to help these people become more firmly established in the faith, and dispel doubts that had clouded their minds because of the false teachings of the feast-keepers. At the end of their missionary tour they were able to thank God that not one member had been lost to these spiritual wolves. Instead, new members had been won to the church. God had been with the missionaries over every lonely, bandit-ridden road. He had preserved their health through mountain cold and valley heat, through mosquito-infested swamp and plague-infested city.

Back home again, Diamondola thrilled her fellow church members by relating experiences of her travels and of visits with members whom she had never met before. She told how some members in Turkey had already laid down their lives through persecution, but many had arisen to replace those whose blood had been shed. In her own bed once more, Diamondola covered herself with her heavy quilt and knelt, with her head bowed on the pillow, and thanked God that He had accepted her dedication and had used her tongue in His service. Little did she realize that this was only the beginning of her work for Him, and that not all of her experiences would end so pleasantly.

## CHAPTER XIII
# *Educational Problems*

*"Give instruction to a wise man, and he will be yet wiser: teach a just man, and he will increase in learning" (Prov. 9:9).*

After her thrilling missionary journey Diamondola was more determined than ever to obtain a high school education. Already she was thirteen and a half, and had had only one year of formal education. It would require many years of toil and expense to realize this ambition. In fact, at the time it appeared almost impossible to fulfill. Father's health was growing gradually worse, and the only source of income was the sale of the silk cloth woven at the looms by Mother and patient twelve-year-old Despina.

But above everything else, Diamondola had learned that summer the value of the education she had already received. She would not have been of much use to the Lord and Elder AcMoody that summer had it not been for the knowledge of English she had acquired at home as she minded the loom. Also, had Father been less diligent in teaching her the Scriptures, she could not have found the Bible texts so readily as she translated for the missionary. Besides these things, Alexandra's stress on memory work had paid off. How faithfully her older sister had worked to teach the little girls hundreds of Bible verses in three languages—English, Turkish, and Greek. As a result, Diamondola could quote many verses from memory.

Now that the advantages of a good education were so apparent, she prayed with all her heart that God would somehow help her to obtain more knowledge. She perhaps could have had enough money for one more year of formal education had she accepted the money that Elder AcMoody wanted to give her for her summer's translating work. But this both she and her family refused. They all felt that God had done so much for them that they could not accept money from the Lord's treasury. Hers had been a labor of love.

One day Elder AcMoody sent word from Constantinople that he was giving Diamondola the privilege of attending the new Adventist mission school in Bardizag, a town about fifty miles northeast of Brousa, near Nicea. Since she had refused to accept remuneration for her summer service, she could attend the school for a year without charge. This was a marvelous opportunity she could not afford to miss. In a few days Diamondola had packed her few belongings and was on her way to Bardizag.

The new school was opened in the home of one of the Adventist sisters. Fifteen pupils between the ages of ten and fifty enrolled. Elder AcMoody was the principal. But the translator and lower grade teacher appointed by the mission never arrived. Asnive Inedjian, the mission appointee, was an Armenian girl, and her ethnic background had posed a problem from the beginning. For several months, there had been trouble between the Turks and the Armenians. The trouble had been the result of open rebellion on the part of the Armenians, brought on by Turkish massacres of Armenian Christians. The Turkish Government, in an effort to bring under control the Armenian minority, restricted their movements to their home area. At first the authorities in Constantinople promised to allow Miss Inedjian to go to Bardizag. They were aware that the Adventists were not involved in plots against the government. But new outbursts of rebellion caused the authorities to cancel all exceptions. As a result, the only solution was for Elder AcMoody to use Diamondola as his interpreter and as teacher for the lower grades.

Diamondola found herself in an unusual position, to say the least. She, a girl of thirteen and a half, with only one year of formal education, was asked to teach pupils who had more years of education than she had. In spite of this handicap, she succeeded in teaching her pupils the three R's to the satisfaction of their parents and the principal. But this was not all.

As soon as her classes were dismissed, she translated for the upper classes, which consisted of English, Bible, and arithmetic. By doing the translating work, however, she found that she was able to master all the upper-grade classwork with very little extra effort. In this manner, the school year was completed successfully, and everyone was pleased with the amount of knowledge he or she had acquired during the year.

A few days after the close of school the students were all saddened to learn that the new school would not reopen the following autumn. Elder AcMoody had contracted tuberculosis, and had to be returned to the United States permanently. Missionaries sent to Turkey did not seem to be able to maintain their health. This was the second missionary casualty.

When Diamondola received this disappointing news, her hopes of obtaining an education were crushed. Back home that summer Diamondola and Despina worked together at the looms and planned their future. Since Father was now a hopeless invalid, one of them must spend full time at home helping Mother make a living. Since Diamondola, now fourteen and a half, was the eldest, Despina, who was thirteen, unselfishly agreed to stay at the loom and work with Mother while Diamondola completed her education. Then, after Diamondola found work, her turn would come to get an education.

But there was one major drawback to this plan. Despina and Mother, working at the looms, could earn only enough to pay for the household needs and Father's medicines and doctor bills. There was no money left over for tuition and books should she enroll in the local American school operated by the Protestants.

Then one day the girls remembered a possibility they had almost overlooked. Each year the American High School offered a tuition-free scholarship to a promising worthy student with high scholastic accomplishments. Alexandra and Susanna had attended this school during the family's more prosperous days, and had left excellent records. Diamondola hoped that since the school knew of the older sisters' abilities they might grant her a scholarship. But Diamondola's request was not granted. She had left Protestantism to become a Sabbatarian, and the scholarship was given instead to another Greek girl.

Diamondola was keenly disappointed by this turn of events. Next, Diamondola decided to write to Brother Baharian, and tell him of her desire to get an education that she might be of more use in the Lord's work. She asked him if he would lend her the money for her tuition, and promised to pay it back as soon as she graduated and obtained employment.

His answer, however, was not encouraging. Because of his many imprisonments and court cases, and because of highway robberies, he simply did not have the money to lend her. The fact that Baharian had no money to lend was easily understandable, but the rest of his letter did not seem to make good sense to her.

Baharian wrote, "I fear, dear little sister Diamondola, that formal education might do you harm. I am fed each day from the Word of God, and educated by the indwelling of the Holy Spirit."

Diamondola knew that these sources of knowledge were of utmost importance, but she still felt that a formal education would enable her better to serve God.

Baharian concluded with these words, "I fear that more education might cause you to become proud, to depend on your own accomplishments, and to lose your Christ-like spirit. I would not want you to lose your dependence upon God."

Diamondola felt sure that she would never lose her dependence upon God, and she felt that it was because of the education she had already secured that she had been able to serve God in the capacity of translator. Diamondola was confident that though Baharian was a man of God, he had missed the mark on the matter of her education.

Keenly disappointed, Diamondola wished that God would remove from her the desire to learn so that her heartbreak would not be so strong. She tried to resign herself to spending her time working at the loom, but the hurt of her disappointment remained. The future of her education seemed dark, yet the hours spent at the loom brought an unexpected blessing.

While the girls cared for the looms, Theodora had time at last to listen to the reasons for Elijah's faith. When she learned that all of his beliefs were founded on the Bible, she accepted the Adventist faith wholeheartedly. She was baptized in the summer of 1908, and became a firm pillar in the church.

That autumn the girls and their mother decided that the girls must study in spite of obstacles. They borrowed books from some of their friends at the American High School and studied English, grammar, geography, and history. A Greek professor, a friend of Father's, came to the home on certain evenings and taught the girls mathematics and ancient Greek.

Despina and Diamondola studied as they wove silk cloth at the looms. The sale of the cloth provided the family with money for their household needs and father's medication, but there was never any extra money to save for future tuition. It was physically impossible for them to work more hours at the looms. However, they did enjoy doing embroidery work in the evenings while they sat on the couch with their feet curled up under them, chatting with Father. If they could only sell their fancywork they would have money to save for tuition.

During the next few weeks the girls took special pains to produce attractive designs on the handkerchiefs, neckties, and fancy collars they embroidered. They also crocheted pieces of lace, and sewed them on colored paper to make attractive displays.

When the girls had accumulated a good supply of their work, they decided to try their hand at selling it. They found ready customers at the homes of the American, French, and English consular officials. Down the street from the Keanides home was a large tourist hotel where they found more people who were glad to buy their goods. After this they went to the American Protestant missionary in Brousa and showed him several dozen pieces of a variety of their work. They asked him to send this work to his church in America and tell the people that the proceeds were for their education. The people in America were evidently touched by the zeal of the girls, and sent back a check for forty gold Turkish pounds. The girls could hardly believe their eyes when the missionary called them to his office to give them the money. How thankful they were to God for opening the way for them to obtain money for an education.

Because of their heavy home-study program, plus their weaving work, they soon found that they did not have time enough in the evenings to prepare all the lace, needlework, and embroidery work they could sell. It was then that the enterprising little merchants decided to expand their business by employing others. They knew many girls and women in Brousa who just idled away their days doing nothing. Many of these people were capable of doing lovely handwork. The Keanides sisters found that these idle ones were happy to earn money doing fancywork. The Keanides girls provided the materials and ordered the designs that they found sold best. Then they had each employee learn a specialty. In this way, each employee became more efficient. The business venture proved to be a success. Before that winter was over, fifteen-year-old Diamondola and thirteen-and-a-half-year-old Despina had a flourishing business.

When school opened in the fall of 1909 Diamondola had enough money to pay for her tuition and books, with a little left over for the next year. With a heart filled with gratitude she paid her fees to the American High School of Brousa, and began registering for the term.

"What grade are you registering for?" asked the principal as she glanced over Diamondola's papers.

H'mm. Diamondola had not thought about that. She dreaded telling them that she had had only a smattering of formal schooling, but that her home study had provided her with a good general knowledge. She dreaded the thought that she might be placed with the elementary grades.

The next day, however, the teachers decided to give all the students examinations to find out just how much they knew in the various subjects, in order to be able to classify them accordingly. The examinations were both oral and written. During the oral examination, she realized that she was becoming the center of attention. The teachers asked her many questions, then went to discuss her case among themselves.

"Are you sure you are telling us the truth about your previous education?" they asked her, when she was again called before the teaching staff.

"Yes," she answered simply, "I am telling the truth. My sister Alexandra, my books, and my God have been my only teachers outside of the year I studied in the Greek Orthodox school and the year I had with Mr. AcMoody two years ago. My father, mother, and friends have all shared their knowledge with me. I do hope that I can make"—she paused a moment— "your high school class of freshmen."

"Yes," the principal assured her with a smile, "you made the freshman class in mathematics and French; and the sophomore class in all sciences, geography, and history. But you simply amaze us with your knowledge of Bible, English, and ancient Greek. We believe you are beyond anything we have to offer here in high school; however, we are going to place you in the junior class in those subjects, and consider you a sophomore student in general. In three years, you should be able to get your diploma easily. We hope this will prove satisfactory to you."

Satisfactory? Well, there must be words in some language to describe Diamondola's joy as she hurried home with the good news. Diamondola was popular with her class. She was intelligent, well-traveled, vivacious, and fun loving. But she also became a spiritual leader in the school, and made outstanding scholastic marks. In spite of the honors heaped upon her she continued to be kind and helpful, and saved her classmates many hours of difficult dictionary work by explaining the English words to them.

The year was passing rapidly and happily for Diamondola. The only shadow that marred her joy was the thought that poor, faithful Despina was at home working and waiting for her turn at formal education. With good fortune, Diamondola would finish high school at eighteen, and then she would find work and send Despina to school. How she loved Despina for her willingness to be the drudge and earn the living while she learned!

At the end of that school year Diamondola would complete her sophomore year of high school, and then she would have only two more years left until she would get her diploma. But before her sixteenth birthday came around in March, 1910, her education was again interrupted. There seemed to be no end to her problems of getting an education.

*CHAPTER XIV*
# The Second Missionary Tour

*"Come over into Macedonia, and help us" (Acts 16:9).*

Two thirds of Diamondola's sophomore year in high school was completed. Diamondola and Despina had worked hard selling handwork pieces to earn the tuition for the education Diamondola was now enjoying. During the evenings after school and work the girls continued to peddle their fancywork in order to save money for tuition for Diamondola's junior year.

In the midst of this promising prospect, a disturbing letter from E. E. Frauchiger, a German-speaking Swiss and the new missionary in Constantinople, arrived for Diamondola. In essence it read: "Sister Diamondola, we desperately need your help at this time. There are reports of an awakening in Greece. Will you please go down to Smyrna and then go to Greece with Brother Greaves as translator?"

Go to Greece? Leave her school now and sacrifice all the credits she had built up to complete her sophomore year? Diamondola considered the request carefully, and decided that to quit school now and go on the missionary journey would not be wise. Surely, the missionary journey could wait until June, when school would be out. When she finally wrote

Elder Frauchiger, she did not reply negatively, but requested a postponement so that she could complete her school year.

Elder Frauchiger received Diamondola's letter, but could not agree with her reasons for postponing the journey. By return mail he told her that the visit to Greece was most urgent, and that he would like her to go down to Smyrna without delay.

Diamondola and her family knew how desperately the mission needed workers who could speak all the languages of the Aegean area—Greek, Turkish, and Armenian. Up to that time, none of the missionaries had been able to stay long enough in the field to become fluent in those languages. The record looked grim: Dr. George had spent from 1903 to 1906 in Turkey, then had to return to the States with a fatal illness; Elder AcMoody had scarcely remained two years, from 1907 to January, 1909, and then had returned because of his health; W. E. Howell had remained in Greece from 1907 to the summer of 1909, when he was called to work in the General Conference. But fortunately, two new missionaries arrived in the meantime.

Early in 1907 R. S. Greaves from Canada entered Turkey and established his headquarters in Smyrna. Then in the summer of 1909 Elder Frauchiger began to work in Constantinople as a director of the Turkish section. Both of the new missionaries were handicapped in that they did not speak the languages fluently. Turkey had always had national workers since Brother Anthony, the Greek shoemaker, had brought the message to Baharian in 1890. Ministers trained by Baharian were bravely preaching the gospel throughout Turkey, but they were all Armenians and therefore their work was circumscribed. In spite of the tight restrictions on the movements of Armenians in Turkey, Baharian, in one way or another, managed to circulate among the Adventist groups and churches in Turkey.

Diamondola realized that neither Elder Greaves nor Elder Frauchiger could make the trip into Greece without a translator. She also knew that the Armenian pastors would not be allowed to travel in or out of Turkey. But how could they ask her to sacrifice her education in order to serve as a translator?

The second letter from Elder Frauchiger worried Diamondola a great deal. Conflicting questions kept popping up in her mind as she pondered the request. Did God want her to go on the missionary journey immediately? or did God want her, most of all, to finish her education? Was God testing her to learn whether she loved His work or her education the most?

Diamondola discussed her problem with some of her teachers at the American High School. They all told her it was absurd to leave school now and lose the whole year. After all, they reasoned, had any of the Adventists offered to pay her way through school? And what were they offering her now in the line of pay? Nothing, absolutely nothing. And that is also what she would end up getting in school. So Diamondola was persuaded to stay in school and finish the year. She reasoned that she would be that much closer to completing her education, and would be much better prepared to work for God if she remained in school for the rest of the school year. Diamondola wrote a second letter to Elder Frauchiger in which she tried to explain her educational problem.

As soon as he received this letter he sent a third, more urgent, letter posthaste, stressing the importance of this missionary journey.

"Please," the letter entreated, "pack your bag and go down to Smyrna immediately. Elder Greaves is waiting for you."

This plea exceedingly distressed Diamondola. *Am I, like Jonah, running away from a God-given responsibility?* she asked herself. *Should I not be more like the submissive Samuel, and say, "Speak, Lord, for thy servant heareth?" When the Lord asked, "Who will go? and whom shall I send?" hadn't Isaiah volunteered, "Lord, send me?" After all, why am I struggling to get an education anyway? Is it not to be of greater service to God? Well, here is a chance to serve God, and I have twice refused.* Conscience-smitten, and submissive, Diamondola packed her old leather suitcase and prepared her bedroll.

The next morning found her aboard the day train headed for Constantinople, since direct passage to Smyrna was unavailable. In Constantinople, she went to Elder Frauchiger's home and volunteered her services. The next day Elder Frauchiger put Diamondola on a steamer bound for Smyrna. As she passed Troas she thought of Paul's vision of the man of Macedonia calling, "Come over and help us." It seemed that God was giving her the same urgent call. On March 12, Elder Greaves and Diamondola took passage for Greece. They crossed the Aegean Sea to Piraeus, the seaport for Athens. From Piraeus, they took the train to Athens, about ten miles to the north, arriving there about three in the afternoon.

Outside of Athens, Diamondola and Elder Greaves found Mr. Sarantis Fameliari, the man with whom the mission had been corresponding. By studying the Bible on his own, Sarantis had been convinced of the Sabbath, which he began to keep in 1903. He knew not that there were other

Sabbath keepers in the world. Finally, he learned that there was a Sabbath keeping church in Constantinople. Subsequently he wrote periodically to the "church that keeps the Sabbath." It was this correspondence that convinced Elder Frauchiger that the missionary journey into Greece could not be postponed until summer. So, it was specifically for this soul, and generally for an investigation of interests in Albania, that this missionary journey was undertaken.

Diamondola and Elder Greaves stayed with this Greek for a week and instructed him in all the principal points of doctrine, even though he was well versed in the Scriptures and prepared for baptism. At the end of this week of instruction, like the eunuch in Philip's experience, the new convert wanted to know, "What doth hinder me to be baptized?"

"Nothing," answered Elder Greaves. "Where is the water?" The Greek brother remembered an ideal spot, well secluded, and only a few miles away at the foot of a mountain. The three made the trek to the baptismal site, where they found the ruins of an old monastery. In front of the monastery was a large stone cistern about nine feet square. A pure stream of water from a mountain spring ran into the cistern and passed out through a hole near the bottom on the opposite end. Formerly, this cistern had been used as a water reservoir by the monks of the monastery. Now the Adventists were using it as a baptistry. By stopping up the hole, they soon had an ample supply of pure, fresh water. Then Elder Greaves solemnly baptized the first Adventist convert in Greece.

As the three Adventists wended their way back up the mountainside, a thrill of holy joy filled each heart. Diamondola felt that the joy she was experiencing was well worth the loss of a year's schoolwork and tuition money. She had helped to win the first soldier for Christ in Greece, and now the banner of the third angel's message was unfurled in a new country. How happy she was that she had heeded God's Macedonian call to her. Surely this was the thing God wanted her to do, and she was satisfied.

Leaving the new convert in Greece, the two missionaries returned to the seaport. The mission wanted them to call on interested ones in Albania. Taking a steamer, they traveled through the isthmus of Corinth and into the Ionian Sea. At last they anchored in Ayia Sarandë on the coast of Albania. There was an Adventist brother, George Brakas, living in Vostina, Albania, and it was to his home that the missionaries first made their way.

After riding fifteen hours on horseback along narrow paths over rugged mountain terrain, they reached Vostina. Elder Greaves knew quite a bit about this man and his family, for he had corresponded freely with him. He had accepted the Adventist message through tracts given him by a colporteur, and later asked for missionaries to be sent to preach in his city. The bigoted priests excommunicated him from his former church and expelled his children from school. The Albanian Adventist family was overjoyed at seeing fellow believers. Tears of gratitude flowed freely as the family embraced the first Adventist minister they had ever seen, and Diamondola. The two missionaries were then invited to hold a series of meetings in their town.

Elder Greaves held his evangelistic meetings in an upstairs room above the small store that the Adventist brother had recently opened. He fixed it up as best he could, using a number of empty petroleum barrels for seats, covering a desk and a few special seats with traveling blankets, and hanging his charts on the wall. Though it was simply furnished it appeared respectable.

Attendance was good and it became necessary to secure more boxes for seating all those who attended, most of whom were Jews and Greeks. Diamondola usually translated Elder Greaves's sermons into Turkish while they were in Albania, since Turkey controlled the Balkans at this time and Turkish was the common language understood by all. After the meetings Diamondola distributed tracts to those who attended. Once she sold a New Testament to a Jew who was interested in studying about Jesus. She also sold a New Testament to a Turk, and a Bible to a government official who was fascinated by the studies.

Good progress was made in this village and much prejudice was broken down. George Brakas, his wife, and daughters were then baptized. They were the first baptized Adventist church members in Albania, and the missionaries went on their way rejoicing. It had been easy to travel in Greece, but Albania was mountainous and backward, and travel was often quite difficult. All trips had to be made on foot, by mule, on horseback, or by buggy. Inns for lodging were not readily available, so that at times the missionaries found it necessary to rent rooms in private homes.

One evening they were unable to reach their destination before nightfall. The mule driver, knowing that the mountainous path ahead of them was treacherous, decided that they would have to stay in the first village they came to. So, he took the missionaries to the home of the village chief, who, like Abraham of old, graciously welcomed these strangers. He hurried to the animal corral and returned with a young kid, which he ordered prepared for the visitors. Elder Greaves begged his host not to trouble himself, saying that they would be most satisfied to eat simply milk and bread. But the hospitable Albanian would not be convinced. It took several hours for the goat to be dressed and cooked and the newly made dough baked on hot coals. Meanwhile the host and the visitors talked. The chief pleaded for Elder Greaves to hold a meeting, even though his humble village was not on their itinerary. Elder Greaves could not but consent to such a plea.

When supper was ready it was spread out on a clean cloth on the floor. There the missionaries partook of a palatable meal of roasted kid, hot bread baked crisp on red-hot coals, boiled fresh milk, butter, and cheese.

After the meal had been cleared away, the local teacher and many of the other villagers came to the meeting. The host had arranged the meeting to be held in his one large room. All listened eagerly as the story of the gospel was unfolded in beautiful simplicity by Elder Greaves, with Diamondola translating. The people wanted to hear more and more, and the meeting went on and on. The weary young translator could hardly keep her eyes open as she repeated in Turkish Elder Greaves's message. Nevertheless, the message was effective and many were turned to God. That evening more tracts were distributed, and another village was opened to the gospel. After the eager listeners had had most of their questions answered, they returned to their homes, and the weary missionaries were at last allowed to retire.

Since there was only one room in the house, it was obvious that the missionaries and the host and his family would have to share the same bedroom. There was a long, low trunk about the length of Diamondola on which Elder Greaves spread out her blankets. He felt concerned for the health of the frail maiden, who was valiantly enduring the hardships of their rugged itinerary. Some days the distances between villages had been great; sometimes they had had to travel long hours on muleback over difficult terrain and alongside fearsome precipices. The hotels, inns, and rooms where they had stayed were frequently inadequate for their needs. The restaurants, when available, were often so unsanitary that they had usually subsisted on bread, cheese, butter, fruits, and nuts, eaten along the roadside.

The morning after their meeting in the home of the village chief they resumed their journey, and on April 13 reached Yanina, their destination.

They found a suitable place, and soon Elder Greaves began holding meetings each night. During the day, he and Diamondola visited from house to house, and extended invitations to the city folks to attend the Bible lectures. The attendance was good, but the laborious schedule began to tell on Diamondola's health. The girl felt starved for some warm cooked food.

One evening as she and Elder Greaves walked toward the meetinghouse they passed a grocery store that had cans of sardines displayed in the window. Diamondola stopped and gazed hungrily at them. Suddenly an overpowering urge to eat cooked sardines overwhelmed her. She asked Elder Greaves to buy her a can of sardines to satisfy her craving before she began to translate. Elder Greaves was a man of firm convictions on the matter of eating clean and unclean meats.

He insisted that sardines were unclean, "Because," he claimed, "they have no scales." Diamondola insisted that they did have scales, that they were clean fish, and that she was faint with hunger.

"No," insisted Elder Greaves, "they are not clean."

"Yes," argued Diamondola equally insistent, "they are clean."

A heated argument ensued right there on the street in front of the grocery store.

"They are clean!"

"They aren't clean!"

"They are!"

"They aren't!"

"Yes!"

"No!"

"I want them!"

"You can't have them!"

At last Diamondola, weak, tired, and still craving sardines, returned to their hotel room while Elder Greaves went on his way to the meeting hall. Tears of shame stung her eyes as she realized that she had given in to anger, and had contradicted a minister of the gospel. What kind of a missionary was she anyway? What must God think of her? But God understood. She repented of her sin, and never again did she rebel against one of God's ministers. How Elder Greaves managed to conduct his meeting without her that night she never knew, for she never asked him, and the subject was never discussed again. After this incident, however, Elder Greaves did try to secure a more adequate diet for his frail little translator. A few nights later Diamondola was waxing eloquent in her translation of Elder Greaves's stirring sermon on the state of the dead, when suddenly she felt an irresistible itch on her scalp. She tried hard to resist the urge to scratch, but couldn't. Finally, while Elder Greaves read from 1 Thessalonians 4:13, Diamondola began scratching. It felt so good she didn't want to stop. When he had finished reading the text, Elder Greaves paused and waited for Diamondola's translation.

Diamondola gave a last quick scratch, and translated the verse from memory, for she had been too busy to find the passage. Brother Greaves continued: "For if we believe that Jesus died and rose again, even so them also which sleep in Jesus will God bring with him." Scratch, scratch, scratch. Suddenly Diamondola felt something slip out from under her fingernail. Whatever it was tried to make a quick getaway under the bun on the top of her head. Making a quick grab, she caught the offending creature between her thumb and index finger.

Elder Greaves read the verse again, and nudged his translator. No response. He cleared his throat loudly as a signal for her to proceed. With her mind still on the creature she began to mumble thoughtlessly, "Even so them also which sleep in Jesus will God bring-bring." With this she gave an extra hard tug on the stubborn louse that clung tenaciously to her hair. "Bring-bring--down." With a yank, she brought down the louse, along with some hair, and began to examine the cause of her discomfort under the lamplight.

"Look, Elder Greaves," she whispered curiously, quite oblivious of the presence of the audience, "look what came out of my hair. What is this creature?" As she said this she held the creature up for his inspection. If Elder Greaves was disturbed by the distraction caused by Diamondola's scratching, he was doubly disturbed when he was called upon to examine the first louse that his translator had ever seen. The situation had to be mastered quickly. Resorting to the minister's tried and true wake-up device, Elder Greaves brought down his hand on his lectern with a resounding clap. Under his large hand was Diamondola's small one, still clutching the offending louse between her finger and thumb. Wrapping his fingers firmly around her hand, he inconspicuously reached under the desk and removed the louse from Diamondola's grasp, crushing it between his fingers.

The slap on the desk startled the audience, and drew their attention back to the speaker and the subject. The slap had a similar effect on the translator, who resisted the urge to scratch her head during the rest of the sermon.

The next morning Elder Greaves and Diamondola began the work of exterminating her crop of lice. Although it was Diamondola's first experience with lice, she had heard of a cure. She had been told that pouring kerosene on the hair and leaving it on for twenty-four hours would kill the lice and their nits. So, Elder Greaves dutifully went to the shop and bought a bottle of kerosene.

Diamondola wrapped a towel around her shoulders and poured the kerosene into the enameled washbasin before her. Then she poured the kerosene onto her hair and scalp and rubbed vigorously. Soon her eyes were smarting and her scalp felt as if it were on fire.

She dropped onto her sleeping mat with a burning sensation in her eyes and scalp. She became nauseated and developed a fever. Elder Greaves became alarmed and urged her to rinse off the kerosene, but she was determined to get rid of the lice. Twenty-four hours later, when the kerosene had all evaporated, Diamondola took soap and water and washed away the foul smell and the dead tenants. Then she combed her long dark-brown hair until she felt that every louse was gone.

Gone was something else, too. Gone were Diamondola's immaturity, impulsiveness, and stubbornness. In their place came responsibility, self-possession, and submissiveness. During the nearly two months of intensive missionary work Diamondola began to learn to blend skill with adaptability, and dignity with humility and wisdom.

The itinerary in Albania was almost over. One day a telegram from Smyrna arrived for Elder Greaves informing him that Mrs. Greaves was desperately ill with typhoid and was not expected to live. So, the missionaries hurriedly packed their few possessions and hired a horse and buggy to hurry them to Preveza, the nearest seaport. Since they were about forty hours' drive from Preveza, they would have to travel day and night in order to catch the steamer that was scheduled to leave in two days.

The second night of the strenuous journey the driver stopped at an inn for food and to get a fresh horse. Diamondola and Elder Greaves also rested briefly and ate some bread and warm milk. Soon the driver and his passengers were back in their seats, and on their way again, racing against time to catch the steamer before it left Preveza. They had gone but a short distance when Elder Greaves remembered something he had left on the lobby desk. He stopped the driver, jumped down from the buggy and raced back toward the inn, saying as he went, "I'll be back in a minute."

Although the inn was not far from where they stopped, it was not visible in the darkness. Diamondola waited in the buggy with the sleepy driver, hoping uneasily that Elder Greaves would really be only a minute. They waited and waited, but no Elder Greaves arrived. By now he had had time to make the trip back and forth to the inn at least three times. The driver was becoming impatient.

Finally, he drove the horse and buggy back to the inn. The innkeeper told the driver that the gentleman had returned to the hotel, retrieved his parcel, and left long ago. Now both Diamondola and the driver were disturbed. What could have happened to Elder Greaves? She had learned to depend on him as a father. Now he was lost—lost somewhere in the dark on some strange road in a country where he could not speak the language. Diamondola urged the driver to help her find her "father" missionary. The driver returned to the place where Elder Greaves had left the carriage. Now Diamondola was alone with the driver. She became tense with fear. Time was slipping by, Elder Greaves still did not appear, and the unsympathetic driver threatened to take Diamondola back to the inn and leave her there.

I'm too weary," he fumed, "to sit here wasting my time waiting for a crazy Canadian running wildly about the country at night. If he doesn't have any better sense than to know that the horse could have run back to the inn faster than he could go, he probably doesn't have a sense of direction either."

Diamondola sat in the carriage, tears streaming down her face. She was shivering from cold and fear, and praying fervently that God would guide Elder Greaves back to the carriage. She trembled as she imagined herself a helpless girl deserted in a lonely inn in Albania. Wild thoughts raced through her mind. Perhaps a robber had assaulted Elder Greaves. Or perhaps he had fallen in the darkness and injured himself so that he couldn't walk. The night was pitch dark, so the driver could not see her tears, but he must have heard her muffled sobs as she poured out her heart to God. God must have heard, and softened the driver's heart, for soon he expressed sympathy for the little Greek maiden who had lost her father.

After more than an hour a shuffling, puffing Elder Greaves stumbled up to the carriage. There was no time to waste on questions and answers now, if they were to get to Preveza on time. Elder Greaves gave Diamondola the word to go, which she passed on to the driver. With a crack of the whip the driver urged the horse on. They arrived in Preveza in time the next morning to get the steamer. A few days later, on May 7, they arrived in Smyrna.

They were happy to find Mrs. Greaves alive and recovering slowly. After reaching Smyrna Diamondola was eager to return home. Soon passage to Constantinople was arranged. The day she left, Elder Greaves pressed into her hand an envelope containing money. "This," said he, "is your wages for the two and a half months you have spent on the missionary tour."

"Oh, no," protested Diamondola. "I cannot take God's money. I was given my room and board all those days, and that was sufficient for my humble services."

But Elder Greaves insisted that she accept the money, saying, "'The workman is worthy of his hire.' You have been a great help to me and the cause of God. God pays His servants from His treasury. When one makes great sacrifices of time and effort, one must be paid a reasonable sum for his services. You would have earned money at the loom had you been home, and besides, your father will need this help. So, you must accept it as from the Lord. God bless you, my daughter, and may you continue faithfully in His service. I believe you have been called into God's service. You have great talent, my child; use it all to the glory of God."

With this understanding Diamondola accepted the money. Then the godly missionary told her good-by as she boarded the ship to Constantinople, still holding in her hand her first pay from the Lord's treasury.

A few days later Diamondola arrived in Constantinople. She hired a carriage to take her out to the mission, where she gave Elder Frauchiger a brief report of the work accomplished on the missionary journey. Then she boarded the train for Brousa, and arrived home on May 17, 1910. There she encouraged the believers in Brousa by her accounts of her second missionary journey. As Elijah Keanides from his sickbed listened to her reports, he was satisfied that his Diamondola was indeed the little gem he had dedicated to the service of God.

CHAPTER XV
# A Work That Prospered at Last

*"And in every work that he began in the service of the house of God, and in the law, and in the commandments, to seek his God, he did it with all his heart, and prospered" (2 Chron. 31:21).*

Diamondola's attention was arrested by the inspired thought-provoking Bible text found in 2 Chronicles 31:21. Every work she had done for God had prospered. Everything, that is, except her education. Would she never fulfill her ambition to complete her high school education? Diamondola had arrived home too late that spring to finish her sophomore year with her classmates. That summer she took her books and studied diligently, hoping that she could take her examinations later. Then if she did well, she hoped the American High School would allow her to enter the junior class that fall.

The summer of 1910 found Diamondola studying beside the loom again as she, Despina, and their mother continued their work of weaving silk. The girls also pursued their fancywork sideline. Their business prospered.

That autumn when school opened, Diamondola easily passed her examinations with God's help. She was promoted to the junior class with the same six girls who had been her classmates the previous school year—a unique distinction. But Diamondola was unique in other ways, too. The other girls were all boarders; Diamondola was the only day student. The other girls were Catholics, Gregorians, and Protestants; she was the only Adventist. Yet the girls all worked and studied together harmoniously.

Diamondola was too busy to help Despina at the looms that winter, but she did cut, baste, and prepare the handwork materials for subletting. She also collected the finished products and paid the workers. Together she and Despina enjoyed making the sales and counting their money. The fancywork sales and the money from Diamondola's missionary journey paid for the tuition and books that year, but it was the work at the looms that fed the family and paid the rent.

Diamondola had made it a practice never to waste time. As a small child, she had learned her Greek and English vocabulary and grammar while working at the looms. Now, since all of her schoolmates were Armenian, she decided to learn Armenian the same way. Her schoolmates gave her a ten-word vocabulary each day, which she mastered during the interval between classes. Languages intrigued Diamondola, and the Lord seemed to have given her the gift and ambition to master them readily.

Diamondola loved all her teachers, but her special friend during her junior year was the Bible teacher, and director of the school, Miss Jillson. In the Bible, they studied Paul's missionary journeys, and Diamondola thrilled as the experiences were recounted.

Diamondola was taking the third year of French that year. Sometimes the teacher became a bit impatient with her students, when their progress was slow. Diamondola had studied French only six months the winter before, whereas the other girls had had two full years, but her talent for languages enabled her easily to keep up with the class. One day the teacher was writing a lesson on the board. She was standing in such a position that Diamondola could not see the board, but the other girls, who were seated on either side of the teacher, were able to copy her writing immediately. The teacher turned and saw Diamondola twisting to this side and that of her chair. The teacher did not realize that she was the cause for her odd behavior, and assumed that she must be up to mischief.

"Why," she asked Diamondola sternly, "are you not up with the class in copying this lesson?"

Continuing her work and without a moment's hesitation, Diamondola answered innocently, "I'm sorry, teacher, but it's because you are not transparent."

Somehow this innocent remark incensed the teacher, who ordered Diamondola to leave the room. Stunned and perplexed, Diamondola obeyed. When the teacher's anger had subsided, she remembered that Diamondola was never impudent or unkind, and realized that she had been so situated as to make it impossible for her to see the blackboard easily. Apologizing for her hasty action, the teacher asked Diamondola to return to her class. Diamondola cheerfully accepted the proffered apologies, and dismissed the incident.

When vacation time arrived, so did a letter from Elder Frauchiger. Diamondola opened the envelope with trembling hands, wondering whether it contained another call to service. It did. This time Elder Frauchiger asked her to come to Constantinople to do secretarial work, translating, and proofreading for the mission. Although her father's health was now failing fast, he said, "Go, my daughter. This call is God's bidding. Remember you are dedicated to Him."

"The translating I can do, but," worried Diamondola, "I am not trained in typing or secretarial work. And proofreading I have never done."

Elijah never ceased to inspire his children with his faith and confidence in God. "Remember, Diamondola, God's biddings are His enablings. Go, and the God of Jacob be with you. If you do this work for God with all your heart, He will prosper you as He has before."

And so Diamondola went to Constantinople, where she did the work assigned her. She soon learned to use the English typewriter by the hunt-and-peck method.

Diamondola evidently performed her work in Elder Frauchiger's office to his satisfaction, for when autumn came he was not willing for her to go back to school.

"Look," he argued, "a complete high school education is not necessary for you to do your work here. Experience is a good teacher, and we've decided that you are just the one for our job. You have educated yourself exceptionally well, and you have done good work for us this summer. Most of the ministers in our field do not have more than an elementary education. You have a gift for learning languages that is more useful to the Lord's work in Turkey than a high school diploma. Please stay on and work with the mission. We can't get along without your translating and writing."

His arguments seemed logical and reasonable, but Diamondola still wanted to get the high school diploma that would be hers after only nine more months of schoolwork. She finally decided to return to Brousa to finish her education, but agreed to continue to do some of the work for the mission by correspondence. Elder Frauchiger agreed to send Diamondola the English manuscripts to be translated into Turkish and Greek and returned to the mission office for printing. Elder Frauchiger also sent her his letters in English to be translated into Turkish or Greek and sent to the various workers. She also translated the workers' letters to Elder Frauchiger into English, and sent them on to him. In this way, she was the mission office secretary in absentia, and the plan proved to be satisfactory.

In the autumn of 1911 the church in Brousa was meeting in the home of one of the Adventist sisters. One Sabbath, Diamondola noticed a visitor at the church service whom she had never seen before. Because Theodora's home was too small for holding church services it had become her custom to invite the visitors home for Sabbath dinner. So, when Theodora learned that the visitor, Ares Aresian, was an Armenian colporteur, she was more than delighted to invite him to her home for dinner.

After dinner Father rested as usual while Despina and Mother cleared the table. Diamondola was left alone in the living room to entertain the young colporteur. Ordinarily, Diamondola was never at a loss for words, but somehow the way the handsome young colporteur looked at her when she glanced up at him made her falter. At last he ventured:

"Miss Diamondola, it was my curiosity and admiration for you that brought me here to Brousa. Of course, I also have Brousa in my canvassing territory," he added hastily.

"But why," asked Diamondola innocently, "were you curious about me?"

"Well," faltered Ares, blushing, and groping for the right words, "I've heard so much about you. You see, last year I attended the new school in Constantinople that was opened specially to train ministers and colporteurs. Occasionally, the teacher mentioned Diamondola Keanides and the missionary trips she had made with Elders AcMoody and Greaves. Up until a few weeks ago I supposed you must be an older maiden lady. But when I visited one of our churches in central Turkey, I saw your picture in the home of one of our church members. You looked so young and small standing there in the picture with the church group. I could hardly believe them when they said that the child beside Elder AcMoody was Diamondola Keanides. And, well," and the young man blushed as he confessed, "I just had to come here and see if you were truly that girl."

"Yes, I am the girl you saw in the picture." Then trying to lead the subject on to something else she said, "I remember when they took that group picture. I think they wanted to send it to the Review and Herald."

"Later you made that rugged trip to Greece and Albania with Elder Greaves, didn't you?" Ares questioned further.

"Yes, I did," Diamondola answered, becoming increasingly more shy and uneasy.

There was an awkward pause. As Ares considered his future, he knew he would try to make her a part of it. He realized he couldn't expect her to share his feelings so soon, so he said, "I want you to know that I greatly admire your courage and faith. I'm sure that God has greater things in store for you. You are pretty, talented, and intelligent. It is seldom one finds all these qualities in ..." At that moment Despina and Mother entered the room, much to Diamondola's relief.

A few days later Ares left for another city. In the meantime, however, Diamondola made sure that another such meeting did not take place.

When Diamondola entered school on Monday the busy routine occupied so much of her time that Ares was almost forgotten. During the winter of 1912 Elder Frauchiger was appointed head of the Levant Union Mission. However, the union was still attached to the Central European Division. The Levant Union Mission comprised the countries now known as Saudi Arabia, Bulgaria, Greece, Turkey, Iran, Iraq, Israel, Jordan, Lebanon, Sudan, Syria, and Egypt. Its headquarters were situated in Constantinople, because this was approximately in the center of the field. Besides, the work had developed more rapidly in this country than in the other countries that made up the union mission. In Armenia and Turkey alone there were well over 200 members, which constituted about half the membership of the whole union. In spite of persecutions the work was growing rapidly. Diamondola looked forward to becoming a full-fledged worker in the union office.

Diamondola's senior year was drawing swiftly to its close. She was still with the same six girls who had been her classmates since her sophomore year.

Finally, the last week of school arrived, and she was given special permission to stay in the dormitory with the other girls to prepare for graduation. There was the usual rush of examinations and marching practice besides the practice for class night. The girls were in a whirl of excitement, and it seemed as though all the events of their young lives were climaxing in one week.

The first of the closing exercises was class night. The last thing on the program was the class prophecy, which one of the teachers had written. "All seven of the girls," she prophesied, "have a great future before them." She gave in detail what each of the first five would do, and then ended with the two who would become the most famous of the class. She prophesied that one would become known in medical circles (the girl became a doctor in a large hospital in America), and Diamondola, she said, would be a missionary, and would perform a special service that only she could do. Little did anyone realize how accurately this prophecy would be fulfilled.

On Sunday morning, the consecration service was held in the Protestant church, and Monday night at the commencement service the girls received their diplomas. Then it was all over. Diamondola's ambition to complete her education had been realized.

## CHAPTER XVI
# *Ever Learning*

*"The simple believeth every word:*
*but the prudent man looketh well to his going" (Prov. 14:15).*

The day after graduation Diamondola could not get out of bed. The strain of the past few weeks of school, plus her mission work, had been too much for her. She was physically and mentally exhausted, and the doctor recommended complete rest for three months. However, Diamondola was impatient to enter the Lord's work. The mission was waiting for her, and now she had to be detained while she regained her health.

She finally decided to heed the doctor's suggestion because the slightest exertion left her weak and perspiring. Friends arranged for her to be sent to help the church in Bardizag, where she had taught school with Elder AcMoody and had won the lasting friendship of the early Adventists there. She found accommodation and lodging with some of her former students and their relatives, and the summer passed quickly. The weather was invigorating, the food delightful, and the association with so many Adventist youth was good for her spirits.

The Adventists of Bardizag were mostly Armenians, and the never-idle Diamondola decided to add the written Armenian grammar to the

Armenian she already spoke. In this way, the summer was not wasted. This made five languages she could speak.

When the autumn of 1912 arrived, Diamondola was again strong and healthy. She was five feet tall and weighed ninety pounds. This was an all-time weight record for Diamondola. She was in good physical condition as she began to work as a full-time mission employee at the Levant Union Mission office in Constantinople.

That same year another group of workers who had attended a workers' training school that was operated from the fall of 1910 to the summer of 1912 were employed by the Levant Union Mission. Ares Aresian had been one of the most promising students in this school. Because he had learned German along with the Bible lessons and was a good typist he was chosen to be the secretary to Elder Frauchiger, the union president.

The Levant Union Mission had grown so much that another officer was added to serve with the president. Carl Voight became the secretary-treasurer and publishing secretary for the union mission. Diamondola became Elder Voight's secretary and also translated the literature. One of her first tasks that autumn was to proofread the book *Steps to Christ* in Armenian. It seemed providential that she had just perfected her grammar in that language during the preceding summer. Providential experiences such as this confirmed her belief that God was directing her life.

Diamondola knew Armenian well enough to translate the book, but she had no idea of how to proofread. She explained this to her new boss. This would be no problem, Elder Voight explained, for he had a book in English that gave instructions. Once again Diamondola became her own teacher. She tried to digest the lessons as quickly as possible so the publishing work would not be held up. As soon as she had taught herself to proofread, she began to work over the manuscript. She completed the whole manuscript in record time, sent it to the press, and then corrected the galley proofs. At last the book was published, and it proved to be one of the best sellers with the colporteurs.

Although there was much work in the office to keep the workers busy during the day, Ares somehow managed to speak occasionally to Diamondola. Besides these occasions, several evenings a week the whole office staff distributed literature and gave Bible studies, at which times Diamondola and Ares saw each other.

Life in the capital city was exciting. There was always a variety in the daily work program, and Diamondola was constantly meeting new people, usually workers passing through the headquarters office. One outstanding new missionary who arrived from France with his Greek wife was Dr. A. J. Girou. He was appointed to go to Smyrna (Izmir) to set up a dental clinic.

While Dr. Girou was waiting in Constantinople for his orientation and government work permits, he spent some time in the University of Constantinople. While there he became acquainted with some of the professors. One of them challenged him to a debate in the university auditorium. The debate was widely advertised and excited considerable interest among the educated people of the city. This was a real opportunity for the Adventists to make their work more widely known. Diamondola and her friends made certain that they got to the auditorium early enough to get a good seat.

Among the curious listeners in the packed auditorium that night was a professor of astronomy of the University of Constantinople, Diran Tcharakian, and his friend Aram E. Ashod. Tcharakian had been an avowed atheist, but Ashod had convinced him that God did exist. These two men followed the debate carefully, noting the points that Dr. Girou used to prove that God is a Supreme Being, to whom all men are obligated for life—both present and future. And just as remarkable as the lecture was Dr. Girou's charitable spirit and Christian appearance. The audience was spellbound with Dr. Girou's logic and presentation, and many were favorably impressed.

At the close of the lecture the professor who had challenged Dr. Girou could not refute his arguments, so the meeting was dismissed without a rebuttal. From that day on Professor Tcharakian was a changed man. The seeds of truth took root in his heart, and in time he became a powerful witness for God.

Diamondola hoped to be able to put Despina in school during the 1912-1913 school year. But that was not to be. Tuition at the American High School of Brousa had to be paid cash in advance, and Diamondola didn't have the necessary money since she had just begun to work.

Alexandra, in England, had graduated from the Caterham Sanitarium the summer of 1911 and would have gone to work to help the family but the mission had asked her to stay on for one more year to take the special course in midwifery at a Jewish hospital near London. This she did, but it was at the sacrifice of Despina's education. Poor, patient, uncomplaining Despina. Diamondola's heart ached for her loving and selfless sister.

*The church members at Bardizak—most of whom were later exiled or fled to other countries.*

Despina had to spend one more year at the looms with Mother, earning the money to pay for the family's food and rent.

In the meantime, Diamondola determined to save enough money that winter to pay for Despina's room, board, and tuition at the American High School in Brousa the following year. She also planned to bring her father and mother to Constantinople to live with her. Time was to prove that Diamondola's ambitions were beyond her pocketbook, but she was young and the difficulties involved in such a venture did not seem insurmountable at the time.

Headquarters for the Levant Mission were established in a rented house in Constantinople. The large central hall on the first floor was used as the church. Five rooms on either side of the large hall were used as mission offices. The second, third, and fourth floors were sublet to non-Adventists. The fifth floor was small and run down, and some of the Adventist workers decided to live in it. Elder Voight and his wife occupied two of these rooms and the kitchen, while Diamondola and Araxie, a young lady colporteur, occupied the other two rooms and a small cubicle that had been for storage, but which the girls refashioned into a bath. In spite of hardships they accepted their long hours of work, meager salaries, and their cramped accommodations as part of the way of life they had chosen.

Diamondola spent many of her hours translating, stenciling, and mimeographing. The Sabbath school lessons had to be translated into Turkish. This may sound like an easy task for a linguist such as Diamondola, but it was not. Many of the church members spoke Turkish, but they could not read it. The Greeks could read their alphabet and written language, and most of the Armenians knew their alphabet and written language. The problem was to reduce the Sabbath school lessons into Turkish, which the Greeks and Armenians both spoke, but which many could not read. In order to solve this problem Diamondola had to translate the Sabbath school lessons and tracts into Turkish, then transliterate her Turkish translation, using Greek letters, for the Greek-speaking people, and the Armenian script for the Armenian-speaking people. It was no easy task to prepare this material. The stencil wax paper used for this work was laid over a smooth slate, then Diamondola traced the words on the wax paper with a steel or slate stylus. She developed a permanent callous on the first joint of the middle finger of her right hand from pressing the stylus.

After the stencils were cut, they had to be mimeographed. Mimeographing in those days was a chore all by itself. The Levant Union Mission possessed an imposing name, but not the latest office equipment. The old machine on which Diamondola mimeographed those early stencils was a temperamental, grinding, start-and-stop ink slinger. The first time Diamondola tried to operate it, she cranked the handle a few times, then stopped to examine the first few sheets. They were perfect! Crank, crank, crank. Suddenly the handle stuck in midair and the ink spurted out all over the place. Diamondola was splattered with ink from head to foot. She stepped back dumfounded, glaring at the nasty, unpredictable thing. The machine just sat there dripping mimeograph ink. Well, she decided, she couldn't get any dirtier, so she might as well clean up the mess and continue her work.

When she finished the mimeographing for the day, she removed what ink she could without injuring her skin too much and left the rest to just wear off. Her clothing, however, was another matter. The dress retained a permanent black polka-dot effect. So, she decided that that garment would be her mimeographing dress. Never again did she completely trust that old machine. Even so, she was splattered with ink by the temperamental machine several times each day. The office staff became used to seeing Diamondola with ink dripping down her face and hands, and dubbed her "the squid" or "ink fish." Diamondola didn't mind, however, for she had a jolly sense of humor.

Araxie, who shared Diamondola's living quarters, sometimes helped her on the mimeograph when there was a deadline to be met. Diamondola was happy for a friend such as Araxie, for they had much in common. Besides being young they were both active, earnest Christians, and both supported aged parents. Both were poor, and had to live conservatively, even miserly, in order to make ends meet.

One day the two girls decided on a new plan to economize. Diamondola remembered that her mother always bought large supplies of dried staples in the autumn, when these commodities were cheaper. Why not do likewise, and in this way have more cash on hand at the end of the year?

"A splendid idea," Araxie agreed enthusiastically. "Let's begin right now. I see a vendor coming down the street with a whole cartful of onions. He must be selling winter onion supplies to the houses."

They hailed the vendor from their fifth-floor window. He stopped and asked them how many kilos of onions they wanted. The girls were puzzled. They didn't have the vaguest idea how many kilos they needed to last them through the winter. So, they asked the vendor how many kilos he thought they needed.

"Oh," he said casually, taking full advantage of their ignorance, "about forty kilos (about eighty-eight pounds) should be enough for you girls."

Diamondola caught her breath. "So much!" she exclaimed. "Yes," he answered evenly as he proceeded to weigh out the onions. "You can use them in lentils, beans, soup, and bread. Most anything you eat tastes better with a little onion—ah, that is," and he eyed the innocent girls appraisingly, "when you know how to cook." Neither girl knew much about cooking and the wily vendor added this bit of sales talk most effectively.

The girls were convinced, and trusting the vendor's calculations, they ordered forty kilos. The vendor weighed out the onions five kilos at a time, and the girls carried them up the five flights of stairs and put them in the corner of their dining room. With each succeeding trip the pile of onions became larger, and it soon became a problem where to put them. They pulled the cupboard out from the wall and piled more onions between the wall and the cupboard. By then the pile of onions had reached unreasonable proportions. The girls wanted to call a halt to the transaction, but the dealer ignored their pleas.

"Twenty-five kilos only? You'll need much more," he assured them as he continued to weigh more and more onions. By now the pile was threatening to spill over the top of the cupboard.

"Thirty kilos," he affirmed as he checked five more kilos off the scale.

"Oh, please, I think that's quite enough," pleaded Diamondola.

"Not yet-thirty-five kilos," he said as he tipped another load off the pan and into Araxie's basket. Araxie dumped them on top of the heap, but the smooth-skinned onions came slithering down. At this rate, they would have little room to store any other supplies for the winter. The cupboard was moved out farther from the wall, and other boxes were piled between the cupboard and the wall, in order to retain their mountain of onions.

Within the next few days the girls bought a year's supply of walnuts and chestnuts, and piled them in cartons on top of their wardrobe in their bedroom.

The girls decided that dried beans were another good staple. They were a good source of protein and could be eaten with dark bread and onions. So, some dried beans were added to their winter supplies.

One day the girls decided to cook dinner while they worked at the office. In the morning, they put a few cups of beans in the huge kettle, with lots of water. They placed these on their kerosene pressure stove. Closing the door behind them, they went down the steps to work, proud of their new brainstorm. By noon the beans should be cooked and they'd have a warm dinner awaiting them. What was their chagrin when they raced up the steps and saw smoke pouring from between the cracks in their door. The kerosene stove had puffed clouds of smoke and soot everywhere, without so much as warming the beans. It took the girls all their extra time for several days to clean up their rooms.

A few weeks passed, and the girls concluded that they were living as economically as possible, though they sometimes had their difficulties. They were learning to cook with onions, but the pile didn't seem to be disappearing nearly as rapidly as the onion vendor had assured them it would.

The girls had planned to use the walnuts and the chestnuts only when winter came, and so the boxes that contained them remained unopened. One day Diamondola noticed big fat grubs crawling down the side of the wardrobe door. She could hardly believe her eyes. Moving closer she opened the wardrobe door and saw worms crawling over the clothing in the wardrobe. The wriggly creatures gave her the shivers. Where could they be coming from? After a careful examination, she finally discovered that the worms were coming down from the region of the chestnut box. She called for Araxie to come and give her moral support, while she dragged up a chair, mounted it, and gingerly handed the carton down to Araxie. Opening the lid, they stared with repugnance on a wriggling, heaving, mass of worms in the chestnut box. They concluded in disgust that though they had decided to wait until winter to enjoy the chestnuts, the worms had not.

"Well, worms or no worms, we'll have our share of these chestnuts too," Araxie announced with determination. "We'll eat nothing but boiled chestnuts until they are gone. The worms can just find their food somewhere else." With that the vengeful Araxie took off her shoes, and gave each worm in sight a resounding whack, which ended his depredations in the chestnut box.

For the next two weeks, the girls' diet consisted entirely of boiled chestnuts. After just a few days their one-item menu became monotonous. In vain Diamondola pleaded with Araxie to include just a little bread and fruit in the diet. Araxie was adamant. At last the chestnuts were eaten up, and with great relief Diamondola threw out the empty box sincerely hoping she would never again have to swallow another boiled chestnut.

A month or so later the girls noticed that something strange was happening to their onions. Instead of decreasing, the pile seemed to be increasing steadily. Investigation showed that the whole batch had sprouted. "Horrors! Now what do we do?" Diamondola asked her companion.

"Have an onion sale, I guess," answered Araxie glumly as she viewed the pile.

Kind friends eventually took pity on the naive pair and purchased some of their horde. Others took pains to explain—too late unfortunately—that root vegetables are best stored in dark places in order to delay sprouting as long as possible. After this episode, the girls resolved that never again would they be so foolish as to believe the word of any vendor. Diamondola learned a great many lessons on housekeeping and economy that year, and at the same time acquired her sixth language.

It happened this way. Diamondola and Mrs. Voight had become good friends, though neither spoke a language the other spoke. Mrs. Voight, who was from Lithuania, spoke only German and Russian, whereas Diamondola spoke English, Armenian, Turkish, French, and Greek. They communicated through a strange conglomeration of all seven languages, plus sign language. They were able to converse about ordinary things, but when they got stuck they would have to call on Elder Voight to help straighten them out.

"Diamondola," Elder Voight said one day, "why don't you learn German? All the circulars that come from our division headquarters are printed in German. Not only that, but most of the visitors that come from the division speak German, and often we need someone to translate for them. Ares is frequently gone with Elder Frauchiger, and we need a second translator. You could be of greater service to us if you spoke German as well as the other languages."

Feeling that this was a call from God, Diamondola bought a German grammar, a German reader, and an English-German dictionary and began to study. While waiting for streetcars or carriages, or walking down the street, she studied German through that winter until she had mastered it. She felt that God had blessed her efforts. But little did she realize how, soon she would be called upon to use this language for Him.

## CHAPTER XVII
# *Diamondola Goes Through the Valley*

*"Blessed are the dead which die in the Lord ... that they may rest from their labours; and their works do follow them" (Rev. 14:13).*

Ares and Diamondola had not seen each other from the autumn of 1911 until the autumn of 1912. Now they were the secretaries in the Levant Union Mission offices. It could have been an ideal setup to carry on a courtship, but both were too busy to spend much time talking. However, they did manage to speak briefly while at the office and when they went together to give Bible studies, so that their friendship was able to develop, but otherwise they had little time for courting. During the winter Ares took a trip with Elder Frauchiger. He sent Diamondola several letters telling about their journeys. He knew that she was interested in missionary journeys; but more than that, he wanted her to know that he was interested in her, too. Ares wisely did not try to rush Diamondola. He knew that she had plans for helping Despina get an education, and did not try to interfere with these plans. Both he and Diamondola were young, and there was plenty of time to let their courtship mature. In the meantime, they both devoted their fullest energies to the finishing of the Lord's work.

In the spring of 1913 Ares and Elder Frauchiger were planning to visit the churches in the Brousa area. Diamondola knew that they would be in her home church over Easter weekend. Suddenly she became distressingly homesick. She asked Ares if he minded if she went in his place as Elder Frauchiger's translator. He didn't, so Diamondola and Ares approached Elder Frauchiger with their proposal. He readily agreed that the change would be all right, and even preferable, since this would give Diamondola an opportunity to go home, as well as have a change of activity for a few days.

Diamondola was elated. She was going home! Elder Frauchiger planned to leave on a Wednesday and would stay almost two weeks. He and Diamondola would hold ten days of revival meetings in one of the homes in Brousa. It seemed incredible—once again she could sleep in her own bed. She could eat Mother's cooking, and how good that would taste after her own attempts at learning the culinary art. In her imagination, she planned just how she would sit by Father's bed and listen to his words of counsel.

On the Sunday before the trip Diamondola felt an overwhelming urge to leave for home before Wednesday. She tried to suppress this urge but it kept returning again and again. Was this a premonition of evil? she questioned. Or was she suddenly more homesick than she liked to admit? At any rate, she got permission from Elder Frauchiger to leave sooner.

Diamondola left Constantinople Monday morning, and arrived at her home that night. The family was happily surprised as Diamondola walked in the door. But the sight of her father took away some of the joy of being home again. He sat listlessly on the sofa, and raised a weak hand in salutation. She hurriedly kissed Mother and Despina, and then seated herself on the sofa beside her pale, thin father. As she kissed his hollow cheek, she noticed that he was feverish. He had been ill with a bad cold since Friday and had eaten nothing. He smiled wanly at Diamondola. He was so proud that she was working for the Lord. As Diamondola looked at him, she realized that his days were numbered. Was this the cause for her urge to go home earlier than planned? She hoped that with her at home he would soon be nursed back to a measure of health, yet as she looked at him, she despaired. She decided to try to feed her father. She felt that if he ate he would begin to regain his strength. He had not eaten for four days, and this was probably why he looked so wasted.

Supper waited on the stove, but before Diamondola touched it, she tried to feed her father. She sat on the sofa beside him and tried to cheer his spirits with stories of her life in Constantinople, while she fed him bite-sized pieces of bread soaked in warm soup. Elijah ate.

"The joy of seeing Diamondola again has made your appetite return, Elijah," Mother said to him. And so it seemed.

Since Mother and Despina had been nursing Father so long, Diamondola argued that it was her turn to nurse him that night. Father said he preferred not to be moved from the sofa, so Diamondola laid a mattress on the floor beside him. She slept some that night, but her father was so restless that her sleep was fitful. Tuesday morning Mother called a doctor. The doctor gave Elijah an injection and left. Toward noon Father seemed to be weakening. He repeated the twenty-third Psalm aloud. As he did so he seemed to linger over the words, "Yea, though I walk through the valley of the shadow of death." Elijah paused for a long moment of meditation and reflection. Then with full assurance and firmer voice he continued, "I will fear no evil: for thou art with me."

When he finished this psalm, he began to sing in a weak, shaky voice:

> "Rock of Ages, cleft for me,
>   Let me hide myself in Thee;
>
> Let the water and the blood,
>   From Thy riven side which flowed,
>
> Be of sin the double cure,
>   Cleanse me from its guilt and power.
>
> When my pilgrimage I close,
>   Victor o'er the last of foes,
>
> When I soar to worlds unknown,
>   See Thee on Thy judgment throne,
>
> Rock of Ages, cleft for me,
>   Let me hide myself in Thee.

The three anxious watchers knew not what to say or do. It seemed almost as if Elijah were conducting his own funeral service.

Soon after, he relaxed and sighed contentedly, "It is good. It is well."

Then he asked to be taken outdoors, because he felt a smothering sensation. Theodora held him on one side while Diamondola held the other, and both helped Elijah to the door. Suddenly his head dropped forward and he sagged to the floor. By a superhuman effort Diamondola lifted her father in her arms and carried him back to the sofa. Despina hurried to call the doctor, who arrived quickly and gave Elijah another injection.

Diamondola sat on a stool by her father's side and watched helplessly. It was evident that Elijah was dying. Susanna and her family were sent for. Despina and Mother stood at the head of the sofa. Diamondola held Elijah's hand, and noticed that his pulse was weakening. At last there was no pulse. Her father, her spiritual counselor, was gone! Father had not been able to contribute to the family income for several years, but he had contributed greatly to the spiritual life of his family and the church members.

Diamondola knew what had to be done next. There were no funeral homes in those days, so she set about preparing her father for burial.

The next day, Wednesday, Elder Frauchiger arrived, and the following day he conducted the funeral service in the Protestant church. The American High School girls, Diamondola's former schoolmates, were dismissed from classes for the day and spent the entire morning plaiting beautiful wreaths of flowers. Elijah's bier was covered with these tokens of love and respect. Then he was laid to his rest in the Protestant cemetery in Brousa.

After the funeral, the family and friends returned to the house. Words of comfort were spoken to the mourners. All through the ordeal Diamondola had maintained a tense composure. But when the last guest left that night, she prayed for release from her pent-up emotions. The tension was broken, and she wept with utter abandon. It was then that she realized for the first time what a wonderful blessing God has given people in the ability to weep. She thanked God for the blessing of tears, and was comforted by the blessed hope that one day she would see her father resurrected.

## CHAPTER XVIII
# Work and War

*"Whatsoever thy hand findeth to do, do it with thy might" (Eccles. 9:10).*

Ten days after the funeral Elder Frauchiger conducted a brief series of evangelistic and revival meetings in the home of one of the church members. Diamondola and Despina did what they could to help.

After these meetings were over, Diamondola returned to Constantinople and her work. Father would have wanted it that way. Since home was still in Brousa, Mother and Despina planned to live on in the rented house and work at the looms until autumn.

It wasn't easy for Diamondola to leave home again so soon after her father's death, but she was glad that she had been able to see her father before he died. The family tried to be sensible about the loss that God had permitted to come to them. During the years when the girls and Theodora had needed Elijah's spiritual counsel, God had kept him alive. Now that the girls had reached maturity, and two were in God's work, they saw that God had been merciful to relieve Elijah of his suffering.

The Adventist work in Turkey was growing, in spite of serious political difficulties, and there was plenty of work in the office to keep Diamondola busy. There was so much work, in fact, that Diamondola would laughingly say, "If I don't do my work with all my might, I'll never get it done."

At this time, various national and ethnic groups throughout the Ottoman Empire were gradually revolting against the oppression of the Turks. Even some of the Turks themselves were not entirely loyal to their despotic government. In 1911 Turkey fought a short war with Italy. In the autumn of 1912, Turkey again became involved in a conflict, this time with Greece, Serbia, Bulgaria, and Montenegro. This struggle became known as the First Balkan War. In 1913 the Second Balkan War broke out. These wars, which involved Greeks and Turks, made life uncertain for the Greek minorities in Turkey, but the Keanides determined to live one day at a time and not to worry about their future.

From the Levant Union Mission office Diamondola found that it was frequently difficult to communicate with Elder Greaves, who had moved to Salonika, Greece. His letters were likewise delayed in their return to the office. In the summer of 1913, the mission extended an invitation to Alexandra to join Elder Greaves and the young church in Salonika. Alexandra, who had just graduated from the special midwifery course, accepted the call and soon sailed for Greece. How the family longed to see her. She had been away from home almost eight years. Since she was so near they felt sure they would see her soon.

When autumn came, Diamondola and Alexandra were able to put Despina in the American High School of Brousa as a boarder. Mother sold the looms and the extra furniture that would not fit into Diamondola's small apartment, and moved in with her daughter in Constantinople. With this move all the members of the once-prosperous Keanides family, with the exception of Susanna, were reduced to room tenants. But never once did they question the leading of God. They were happy to be poor in this world's goods if they could only help in God's work. Whatever task God gave them to do, they were willing to do cheerfully to the best of their ability.

Conditions had hardly become settled when trouble broke in Brousa. Stavro Xanthopoulos, Susanna's husband, had a thriving barbering business in Brousa because he was neat, efficient, and honest, while other barbers enjoyed only average trade. As a result, they became envious and plotted to get rid of him so they could have his customers. Although this envy had existed for some years before 1913, the barbers could find no pretext by which to rid themselves of Stavro. With the coming of the Second Balkan War, a pretext presented itself. The envious barbers filed an accusation to the government in Constantinople against Stavro, in which it was declared that there was a Greek barber in Brousa who was plotting with the Greek Government against Turkey. The accusation was preposterous, and would have been immediately dismissed had it been filed in Brousa, where Stavro was known as a loyal Turkish citizen. But the officials in Constantinople, unaware of the true situation, viewed seriously the least suspicion of disloyalty. Because of this attitude persons falsely accused were sometimes put to death before an involved trial could prove their innocence.

One day a Turkish police sergeant, one of Stavro's regular customers, entered his barbershop and quietly slipped a message to Stavro saying that he must flee from Brousa that night or he would be arrested. So Stavro, thankful to his Moslem friend, immediately fled to Constantinople. There he looked up Diamondola, who hid him in her apartment. However, the danger of his being discovered was great, so in a few days he fled across the border into northern Greece, then down the coast to Salonika, where Alexandra was working. Susanna knew Stavro's destination, and as soon as she was able, she sold what she could of her belongings without arousing suspicion, and then went to Greece with her two sons.

Alexandra was happy to see Susanna again after the years of absence. She was more than willing to help Susanna and Stavro get established, but it meant that she could no longer help Diamondola support her mother and Despina.

That autumn things had not worked out very well for Alexandra with her work in Salonika. She had spent several months during the summer of 1913 trying to find work in Salonika as a midwife or nurse, but without success. The mission had continued to pay her a regular salary, but she felt guilty in accepting it when she had not been able to render service in the line for which she had been trained. Finally, after several months of searching, a large hospital in Salonika invited her to join its staff as head matron. The Balkan Wars were filling the hospitals with wounded, and more trained personnel were needed. Elder Greaves agreed that it would be good for Alexandra to take this position, as he felt that she would find many opportunities to witness for Christ. This proved to be the case. The hospital appreciated Alexandra's work[2] so much that soon there were

---

2    At the end of the Balkan Wars, Alexandra was decorated by the Greek Government. At the close of World War I, the Allied government also decorated Alexandra for her outstanding services. Alexandra treasured the decoration, but she believed that a greater reward (eternity) and decoration (a crown of jewels) awaited her in God's kingdom. She gave her services to Greece because of her love for God and humanity, not for decorations and honor; but sometimes one receives a double blessing.

extra calls for her services, such as special duty, night work, house calls, and deliveries. In a short time, her hospital income was more than double her mission salary. She could easily have used the extra money she earned to help Susanna and her husband, or Theodora and the girls, but the thought never entered her mind. Instead, she faithfully turned over this entire salary to the mission office, and received only her regular mission salary. She was wholly dedicated to the cause of God, and was happy that her extra money could be used to support the Lord's work in other places.

Meanwhile, Turkey was having her problems securing medical help for her wounded soldiers. The Balkan Wars had also filled the Turkish hospitals with casualties. When the hospitals of Constantinople overflowed with wounded men, the government closed the schools and turned them into emergency hospitals. Dr. Dodd, an American missionary from Iconium, was asked by the Red Cross to transfer his entire staff to Constantinople. They were assigned the Vera School, which was to be operated as an emergency hospital. Even so, the Red Cross and Red Crescent (the Moslem equivalent of the Red Cross) needed space and nurses. Dr. Peet, of the American Bible Society, came to the Adventists for volunteers. He was acquainted with Diamondola's linguistic gifts and her abilities as a home nurse, so he asked Elder Voight to release her for the duration of the emergency. Elder Voight could hardly spare Diamondola, but he also recognized the humanitarian need for her services. Consequently, she was released, and the next day went to work in the hospital.

She was dressed as an ordinary nurse, with gown and cap, and carried the special passes issued by the government to all hospital personnel. This pass, stamped with her name, address, and photograph, entitled her to free transportation on any tram, bus, or ferry boat. It was to come in handy several years later in helping her to remain in Turkey.

Diamondola loved nursing. She almost wished that she had followed in Alexandra's footsteps and that this nursing stint might become a permanent occupation. She soon became so efficient that she was transferred from the soldiers' ward to the officers' ward. The promotion made no difference to her for she liked both places equally well. All the wounded men needed help, and it made her happy to feel that she could do something to relieve their suffering. Diamondola enjoyed her work in the officers' ward—if one can call such heart-rending work enjoyable. Here was a need, and she was glad that she could lend her heart and hand in loving service. One of the officers had a badly mangled leg, which he complained was always cold. One day Diamondola noticed that it was turning black, and had a peculiar putrid odor—a sure sign of gangrene. The doctor ordered surgery, and Diamondola was asked to assist. *Oh, no!* she thought desperately. *I don't want to see an amputation!* Although work at the hospital had hardened Diamondola to repulsive sights, she felt that she was hardly prepared to assist in an amputation.

Yet, robotlike she obeyed, and prepared herself to assist in the operation. The whole gruesome ordeal was almost too much for her. After what seemed hours, the doctor pulled the flesh and skin down over the stump of bone and sewed them neatly together. Then an orderly wheeled the patient back to his ward, while Diamondola stumbled along beside the stretcher.

After a while Diamondola learned to endure the sights and sounds of the hospital, but she was never able to steel herself against the natural feelings of sympathy in the face of human suffering.

One officer was paralyzed from his neck on down. Since he could not use his arms, a nurse had to feed him. Diamondola was so gentle and tender that he always asked for her to help him.

One day as she was feeding him, he smiled gratefully, mumbled a word, and died before her eyes.

The Balkan Wars ended the latter part of 1913, and the civilians employed by the hospital were released and allowed to return to their former employment. Diamondola returned to her work in the office. Years later, this period of service was to save her from expatriation.

## CHAPTER XIX
# *Finding a Good Thing*

> *"Whoso findeth a wife findeth a good thing,
> and obtaineth favour of the Lord" (Prov. 18:22).*

During those busy months at the hospital, Diamondola had seen very little of Ares, but that was not her only concern. Theodora had suffered from loneliness during the many hours she had spent at the hospital, and this weighed on Diamondola. Besides, the work at the office had piled up in her absence. Only the most urgent matters had been attended to.

During Diamondola's absence from the office two used typewriters had been purchased to help her in her work. One typewriter had Greek type and the other had Armenian. Diamondola found that her hunt-and-peck method of typing was considerably easier on the fingers, as well as faster, than her former method of cutting stencils.

Diamondola was happy to be back at her old job, and Elder Voight, whose energetic, intelligent, and tireless promotion had made the publishing work self-sustaining, was also glad to see her back. He had Diamondola translate books and tracts into various languages, which he sent out to publishing concerns in the city to be printed. The colporteurs sold this literature, sent in the money to Elder Voight, who then published more books and tracts. He had the business ability to run a mission poor in financial resources, and still keep it out of debt. As a matter of fact, the publishing work was actually making money to help support the ministry. Diamondola often worked twelve hours during the day in the office, and then gave Bible studies at night. Sometimes she gave the studies herself, and at times translated for others. Ares was doing the same kind of work in other parts of the city.

Mrs. Voight noticed how hard the mission workers labored, and felt that she was contributing little to the Lord's work. She insisted on sewing all of Diamondola's clothing. "Maybe my hours of sewing for you, so that you can spend more time saving souls, will be imputed to me," she said sweetly to Diamondola one day, and Diamondola knew she meant it. Mrs. Voight felt that this was one way she could contribute to the work of God.

Elder Voight seemed so different from his wife. Diamondola noticed that he sometimes seemed careless in his observance of Sabbath. One day Mrs. Voight tearfully confided to Diamondola that she was concerned about Carl's attitude toward the Spirit of Prophecy.

Motion pictures were a new thing in Constantinople in 1914. They aroused everyone's curiosity. One day Elder Voight invited Diamondola and Araxie to accompany him and his wife to a movie theater. The girls accepted the invitation without raising any questions. After all, Elder Voight was a minister. They enjoyed the relaxation from their strenuous schedule so much that the four decided to attend the motion picture theater every week.

Yet, somehow it didn't seem just right to invite Elder and Mrs. Frauchiger and their family to join them. Ares wasn't invited to go either. In fact, Diamondola never told him she went. She wrestled with the question of whether theaters were the place for Adventists to be. But as each Saturday night rolled around, she found herself at the motion picture theater with Araxie and the Voights. Somehow Mrs. Voight didn't seem to share the enthusiasm of the others for the theater, yet she never raised her voice in protest, at least not where Diamondola could hear.

In the spring of 1914, Ares, who was from Iconium, made a mission trip with Elder Frauchiger throughout all of Anatolia.

While on that trip Ares wrote faithfully to Diamondola. His letters became progressively more romantic, and she knew that at twenty-three he was becoming interested in her as more than a casual friend. He frankly admitted in his letters that he missed her.

Before long Diamondola found herself thinking more and more of Ares. His absence seemed to strengthen her growing affection for him. As her love developed, she prayed earnestly. about the matter, and sought counsel from those whom she trusted. Everyone seemed favorable toward the match. In fact, some wondered why Diamondola was so slow to realize that she and Ares were made for each other.

Late that spring Ares returned to Constantinople. He became a frequent visitor at Diamondola's apartment. Mother, who chaperoned them, approved of Ares. When Diamondola accepted a costly and lovely deep-piled carpet, she knew that his next visit would likely bring a proposal. It seemed almost too good to be true. She had often wondered whether she would ever get married, with all the heavy responsibilities that had been laid upon her. But God seemed to be leading them to each other.

The evening after she had received his lovely gift, Ares called. He took her hand gently in his and asked her simply, "Will you marry me, Diamondola?"

Looking up into his serious face, she answered, "Yes, Ares, if I can continue in God's work."

*CHAPTER XX*
# The War to End War

*"And ye shall hear of wars and rumours of wars: see that ye be not troubled: for all these things must come to pass, but the end is not yet" (Matt. 24:6).*

During the few months following their engagement, Ares and Diamondola enjoyed perfect joy while the rest of the world seethed with unrest. The smaller nations felt exploited by the larger nations, while the larger nations were suspicious of one another's power. Rumors of war were rampant during the early part of the summer of 1914.

In June, Despina arrived in Constantinople from her school in Brousa. She brought disturbing news. That spring one of the Moslem girls had been converted to Protestantism. The Moslem government officials from the education department had become so angry that the school was officially closed. The Keanides were now confronted with another crisis. How was Despina to continue her education? Alexandra soon solved the problem. She enrolled Despina in the nursing school of the hospital of which she was matron. Despina had always been interested in nursing, and as she was nearing her nineteenth birthday she was eager to get on with her chosen career. She had not had the educational advantages that Alexandra and Susanna and even Diamondola had had. Despina still had years of high school to complete. At Salonika, she could get her nursing diploma in three years. She came to Constantinople for a few weeks and then left for Salonika and her sister Alexandra. Diamondola was sad to see her go.

One day not long after Despina had left, Elder Voight called Diamondola and Ares to his office. He told them that he had a serious matter to discuss with them. They thought they were ready for anything, but they were hardly prepared for the bolt that struck them.

Voight told them he was leaving the work. He said that he had come to doubt many things taught in the Bible and the Spirit of Prophecy. The Bible, he felt, was a crutch for the simpleminded. Intelligent people like himself needed a deeper philosophy. Point by point he outlined his reasons and arguments for his disbelief in the Bible and the Spirit of Prophecy. In conclusion, he told them that he had written to the Central European Division office tendering his resignation. He said he would be leaving soon and he wanted to tell Ares and Diamondola, whom he sincerely loved, why he was leaving.

Ares and Diamondola sat stunned and speechless. Voight was a capable and highly intelligent man—a man who had accomplished more in two years than others could have accomplished in ten. As soon as Ares recovered from his shock he said, "My dear brother, why have you fallen into disbelief like this? If your reasoning is sound, what do you propose I should follow as a basis for my life? What do you have that is better than the doctrines taught by Seventh-day Adventists?"

Voight answered with manifest sincerity, "I shall base my life on philosophy and reason. I shall learn why all these things are, and I shall come to a conclusion one day."

The thought flashed through Diamondola's mind that this line of reasoning was something like the rationalizing that had caused Lucifer's downfall. It frightened her. If Carl Voight persisted in this course he would be lost—eternally lost. This thought involuntarily brought tears to her eyes. Ares and Diamondola loved and admired Voight. They wanted him to be saved too. Did intelligent minds need something better? If there was something better, Diamondola wanted it too.

"Please, Brother Voight," she faltered at last, "if you ever find a better faith, or philosophy as you call it, tell me, because I will want it too." Voight promised he would, but he never fulfilled his promise.

Carl Voight and his wife returned to Germany, leaving behind them two confused and discouraged young people. The two spent many hours together in Diamondola's apartment, quietly studying the fundamental beliefs of Adventism. Without telling Theodora Keanides why they were doing so, in order not to upset her faith, they searched the Scriptures diligently. When they came to a difficult point, they knelt and prayed until it became clear to them. At last they reached the conclusion that there was nothing better than what they already believed, and they decided to stay with it. This experience strengthened their faith, and they became all the more convinced that the Bible and the Spirit of Prophecy writings were the word of God.

This problem was scarcely settled when Ares and Diamondola faced another crisis. One day early in June, 1914, Gavrillo Prinzip, a young Serbian terrorist, assassinated Archduke Francis Ferdinand, heir apparent to the Austro-Hungarian empire, and touched off the first world war. By August the Allied powers, consisting of Serbia, Russia, Belgium, France, England, and Japan, were at war with the Central Powers, which consisted of Germany and Austria. Turkey and Bulgaria joined Germany, turning much of Europe, and at times even Asia, into a battlefield.

With Carl Voight gone from the office, and with little chance of a replacement for him because of war, Ares and Diamondola had to bear more of the burden than ever before. As the war began to hinder the progress of the Levant Union Mission, the church was at a loss to know just how to cope with the situation. Since Turkey had joined the Central Powers, but the rest of the nations in the Levant Union Mission were inclined toward the Allies, it seemed that the union would have to be reorganized in order to function properly. In Greece, the situation was so unsettled that Elder Greaves was asked to leave, and Alexandra was left to carry on alone. The mission headquarters in Constantinople began to have less and less contact with the division headquarters in Europe. These were trying times. George Keough, an Englishman, headed the work in Egypt; F. F. Oster was pioneering in Iran; Palestine, Syria, and Mesopotamia were organized under the leadership of W. K. Ising; and Zadour Baharian directed the work in Turkey and Armenia. The exact membership of the entire union at this time was not definitely known, but Elder Baharian estimated that at the end of 1914 there were 350 members in 22 churches in Turkey and Armenia.

In the early fall of that year rumors of a prolonged war led Mother Keanides to lay in a large supply of rice and canned milk. This proved to be providential.

The Adventists in Constantinople watched with intense interest Turkey's involvement in the war on the side of the Central Powers and the Allied threat to the Dardanelles. The rest of the world hoped for an early armistice, but Theodora foresaw a long-drawn-out struggle that would last for several years—perhaps until the Lord came. With this thought in mind she stored more milk and rice, which she hoped would last two years or more. When the Voights left, their apartment was taken over by Diamondola and her mother, who used it for storing her supplies of food.

Diamondola hated to think that the war might possibly last for two years, but she never questioned her mother's good judgment.

One day Diamondola decided that she wanted to learn more about housekeeping. If time should last, she wanted to be a good housewife for Ares. But Ares assured her that she need not worry. They would keep their mothers with them in their home, and they would do the housekeeping while Diamondola worked.

In the fall of 1914 disturbing rumors began to filter into Constantinople. It was reported that Christians in the interior of Turkey were being deported into the Syrian Desert.

Turkey was in the throes of the First World War, and Christians were suspected of being traitors to the national cause. The Turks so feared that Christians would sabotage their war effort that they had no Christians in their armies at this time. Their German allies advised the Turks to remove all suspicious Christians from the vicinity of important railroad centers. The Turks sought out these hapless Christians and gave them two hours to pack a small bundle for their trek of several hundred miles east into the Syrian Desert. In most cases a quick death would have been far more merciful. The Adventist believers in the cities along the railroads sent an urgent message to the mission for help. If the mission could just furnish papers guaranteeing that Seventh-day Adventists were connected with Adventist churches in Germany, it was hoped that this connection might cause the Turks to give them special consideration. But the Turks argued that they could not distinguish a loyal Christian from ones who might work against the Turkish Government. As a result, the innocent suffered with the guilty.

On November 3, 1914, the British bombarded the Dardanelles. In order to relieve pressure on the eastern front, two German warships hoisted the Turkish flag and sailed into the Dardanelles, with the British Navy in hot pursuit. The Turks closed the straits but the British opened them up for a short time. While the straits were being opened up, the German warships sped up the Bosporus and into the Black Sea, where, still flying the Turkish flag, they bombarded some Russian cities. As a result, the Russians retaliated against Turkey.

Some of the Armenians in Armenia joined with the Russians in attacking Turkey. They felt that Russia, being a Christian country, would rescue the Armenians in Turkey in return for Armenian support. However, this only caused the loyal Armenians in Turkey to suffer more severely than they would have otherwise.

The war news was discouraging, but the progress of the work of God was in many ways heartening. Those members who were deported and massacred had been faithful unto death. Their blood had not been shed in vain. Because of their courage in the face of death, many others were led to inquire about the hope that sustained these Adventists to their hour of death. Even so, more Adventists were dying than new ones were being added to the church.

One Sabbath day an obviously well-educated man sat on the back row of the meeting hall in Constantinople. Diamondola watched his face as she translated Elder Frauchiger's sermon. He seemed to be drinking in every word. After the meeting, she learned that the stranger was Diran Tcharakian, professor of astronomy at one of the large universities in Constantinople. Though he belonged to the higher class, Professor Tcharakian had come as a humble learner. Laying aside his intellectual superiority, he inquired about the Advent message with childlike eagerness.

After answering many questions, and inviting Professor Tcharakian to come to the services every Sabbath morning and every Wednesday night, Elder Frauchiger could contain his curiosity no longer. "What brought you here, and how did you find our obscure meeting hall, Professor Tcharakian?" he inquired.

Professor Tcharakian smiled and looked a bit embarrassed. "Well, I think the Holy Spirit has been trying to lead me to you for a long time, but I've been slow to obey. My story begins a few years back. A fellow professor, who was an artist and a sculptor, left to work in Egypt a number of years ago. There he learned of Seventh-day Adventists and became associated with a Britisher named George Keough, one of your missionaries. My friend, Mr. Bezirdjian, became especially interested in the books of Ellen G. White, an American writer. He sent me many of her books. I glanced through them, and by looking at the pictures I saw that they were religious books. Until a few years ago I was a confirmed atheist, but one of my neighborhood friends, Aram Ashod, convinced me that there is a God. Sometime after this, Ashod and I attended a lecture given by Dr. Girou in the university auditorium. He convinced me of God's omnipotence, omniscience, and omnipresence. Only a short time before, I had joined the Armenian Orthodox Church, so when Bezirdjian's books arrived, I did not want to read them and get my mind confused. But God wouldn't let me alone. He sent one of your colporteurs, Nicolos Tefronides, to my home last week. He presented one book after another from his brief case. Each time I showed him that I had the book in my library. Then that godly man, in a kindly, courteous manner that spoke straight to my heart, said, 'My friend, if you have all these books, I am surprised you still smoke cigars!' I was so embarrassed that I quickly put out my cigar and discarded the offending tobacco. I knew at that moment that smoking was offensive to God. I also knew I had to learn what was in those books on my shelves, and that they would lead me into a better, more satisfying way of life. Mr. Tefronides invited me to attend the meeting hall at this address. I will admit," the professor added with a twinkle in his eye, "that I had a little difficulty in finding your place, because I was looking for an impressive church; but I got here just the same, thank God!"

"Thank God," added Elder Frauchiger fervently.

"This is just what my heart has been yearning for," the professor continued. "I have all I need of this world's goods, and social standing as well, but they do not satisfy a man's spiritual needs. I thought I had need of nothing until last week, when that colporteur called my attention to the vacuum in my life. I felt a sudden urge to learn what I must do to be saved. After the colporteur left, I went directly to my bookshelves. I pulled out the first book and began to study it carefully. I am now on my second book. I only regret I didn't read them years ago."

From that Sabbath on, Professor Tcharakian occupied a front pew in the little Adventist meeting hall, and was one of the most attentive listeners. He also attended the prayer service held before Sabbath School each Sabbath morning. His heartfelt prayers always brought tears to the eyes of those in attendance, for when Professor Tcharakian prayed, God's presence seemed very near. It was evident that he understood the power of prevailing prayer. There was nothing too hard for Tcharakian's God, and he practiced the verse literally which says that we should come boldly to the throne of God. Yet his boldness was clothed in the utmost humility and reverence.

As Professor Tcharakian grew in grace, he became a symbol to Diamondola of courage and faith.

Just before Christmas of that year (1914) Paul Bridde, a young German bachelor, came to the office to take Carl Voight's place. This relieved Diamondola of some of the extra burden she had been carrying since the departure of the Voights. Brother Bridde did the bookkeeping and publishing work at the presses, while she continued typing her translations of our publications. She was able to work fluently now in Turkish, Greek, Armenian, English, French, and German. The first three of these languages are largely unrelated, but since she had a facility for learning foreign languages, her work was not too difficult for her.

Near the end of 1914 Elder Baharian visited. the believers in Constantinople, and lifted their spirits with his irrepressible enthusiasm. Elder Baharian's wife and family lived in Constantinople, but he was so constantly traveling on missionary journeys that they saw little of him. As the leader of the work in the Turkish section of the Levant Union, he spent most of his time, like Paul of old, traveling from city to city in Asia Minor building up churches, baptizing new members, and strengthening the believers. During the last few weeks of that eventful year Elder Baharian held evangelistic meetings as well as revival meetings in the humble Adventist meeting place. Professor Tcharakian brought many of his friends to hear the wonderful truth he had learned to love. Diamondola and Ares brought their Bible students.

Elder Baharian had a large baptism, and the harvest of souls for the year was outstanding. Even so, though 1914 showed a loss of membership because of the deportations and massacres, the number of those baptized broke all records. The Turkish Adventist believers, both old and new, looked forward with renewed faith to their Saviour's soon return. The war, which brought despair to millions, brought hope to the Adventists, who believed that this was one of the last signs that Jesus' coming was imminent.

## CHAPTER XXI
# *Farewell! Forever?*

*"And when we had taken our leave one of another, we took ship; and they returned home again" (Acts 21:6).*

Winter snows lay over Constantinople, but its soft white mantle did not bring peace to the hearts of the inhabitants. The war news was disturbing. Turkey and Germany had hoped for an easy victory, but as nation after nation joined the Allies, this hope became dimmer and dimmer. Homes in Turkey were broken up as fathers and sons were conscripted into the service of their country. The war department began to look for more men, and the age limit was expanded to include those between the ages of twenty-one and forty. Even Christian Turkish citizens were drafted, including Armenians. University professors had been left to carry on their work, but soon even the younger teachers were called to the colors. Professor Tcharakian, along with other intellectuals within the specified age bracket, had to step down from his professor's chair and don an army officer's uniform.

Diamondola and the other church members did not like to see their beloved professor leave for the army, but he was conscripted nevertheless. Though still not a baptized member of the church, Diamondola knew that

Tcharakian would always obey God to the best of his understanding. His heart of love and compassion would never allow him to murder another man, even though he was an enemy. She promised to write him and send him any new literature that might be published, as well as the Sabbath School lessons.

Soon Diamondola and the mission office heard from Professor Tcharakian. He was stationed in Adrianople, a city near the eastern Greek border. His letters radiated enthusiasm for the truth. He frequently asked for literature to distribute among his fellow soldiers. In one letter, he requested that literature be sent to his old friend, Aram E. Ashod, who was serving as a private in the Turkish Army in Kirkilizi, Bulgaria. He wrote that Ashod thought he was crazy because he was following the Jewish Sabbath. In response Diamondola sent Ashod literature on the Sabbath question.

Professor Tcharakian wrote that one day, while he was moving from one barracks to another on the other side of town, he hired a porter to carry his luggage. Halfway to the new location the porter made off with his valise and completely disappeared. Among other things, the valise contained Adventist literature and his correspondence with Diamondola. He tried to console himself that the letters and the literature would do the thief some good.

"He stole the truth, and I hope the truth will free him from his sins," Tcharakian mused, ever trying to see the brighter side of a situation.

Unfortunately, Tcharakian's wistful musings did not end up as he had hoped. Instead of being converted, the thief turned over the contents of that valise to the Turkish authorities in another city. As a result, less than six months later Diamondola was charged with treason. But at the time all this was mercifully veiled from her.

The rumors of deportations and massacres in the interior of Turkey became more frightening each day. When it became increasingly difficult to contact the members, Diamondola suspected that they, too, had been deported, massacred, or that her letters were being intercepted by the authorities. She felt certain that many of the Sabbath School lessons never reached their addresses, and that her letters were probably handled with little more care. About this time messages reached the office by word of mouth, and occasionally through letters by private carrier, telling of the suffering and atrocities being committed against the Adventists in the interior. Diamondola's heart ached for them all, but especially for the Armenian Adventists, many of whom she knew personally. Many of the families who had entertained her in their comfortable homes while she was on her first missionary journey with Elder AcMoody eight years before, were now lying dead on the roads and hillsides. Vultures and wild animals devoured their flesh, and only God knew where the bones of these saints were scattered.

Diamondola realized that more trouble lay ahead for the Christians of Turkey, but there was nothing she could do about it. She knew that it was only a matter of time before deportation and exile would come to Constantinople. Ares, a healthy young man of twenty-four would surely be conscripted. During the winter months, other Protestant ministers had been called to the army, and Ares would probably be no exception.

Spring came, and with it urgent messages from Alexandra in Salonika. Since the war had caused the departure of Elder Greaves from Greece, she had been left alone to bear the burdens of the work. She begged Elder Frauchiger to send her pastoral help. Frauchiger studied the problem from all angles, and finally reached a decision. Although they were burdened in the office, it hardly seemed fair to leave Alexandra alone in Greece. So, after much prayer and deliberation, Elder Frauchiger decided to send Ares, his capable office assistant, and the most promising young minister in Constantinople, to Salonika. Elder Frauchiger knew that as a result he and Diamondola would have to stretch their strength to the limit to keep up with the mission work, but with Brother Bridde there to help them, they thought they could manage. The arrangement, however, was only to be temporary.

Ares was happy for the new assignment and the challenge it presented. At the same time, he knew he would miss Diamondola. At one time the idea struck him, Why not marry Diamondola now and take her with him? In this way, she and her mother, and he and his mother, would be united with the other Keanides girls in Greece. At first it seemed like a perfect arrangement, but as the young couple discussed these exciting plans, the burden of the Lord's work fell upon them. They realized that Elder Frauchiger could spare only one of them from the office. With Ares gone, there would be no one to do the translating, the secretarial work, and the mimeographing except Diamondola. So, the two young workers sacrificed their personal desires to the interests of the work of God. They decided to lay aside for the time being their plans of marrying right away. Instead, they agreed that as soon as the war was over, Ares would return to Constantinople, and that then they would be married. After that they would again work together in the mission office, while the mothers kept house for them.

In the meantime, Ares would throw his heart and soul into the work in Greece. The war had produced many problems for the Adventists there. As a man, Ares could more easily bear the burden of the ministerial work, and at the same time help with the problems our young men faced when they were conscripted.

As Ares thought of leaving Diamondola, he wanted to give her a parting gift that she could always treasure—something she really wanted. He knew of her love for music and of her desire to have a piano. Heretofore this had been out of the question for her. With his meager salary, he could not possibly save the twenty gold pounds he would need to buy even a secondhand piano. He prayed about the matter, and asked God to help him know what to purchase that would be within his budget. He wanted to buy her something that she would enjoy and that at the same time would be practical.

One day as Ares was walking across a busy thoroughfare he saw a small leather purse lying in the middle of the street. He picked it up and examined its contents. It had no name, no address, no identification whatever—just seventeen gold pounds. He watched the newspapers to see whether someone would advertise for the lost purse, but no mention of it appeared, and after waiting a reasonable length of time, he decided to look for a secondhand piano.

He found just what he thought would please Diamondola—an instrument with excellent tone and in perfect condition, for only eighteen Turkish gold pounds. How thrilled Diamondola was to discover it in her apartment when she came home from work! It was just what she had always wanted. She felt that God must have led Ares to buy this gift for her. Such pure unselfish love, both for her and God, made her love Ares more than ever.

Diamondola hated to see the day of Ares' departure draw near. She was partly consoled by the fact that Ares would be seeing her sisters. But she longed to be with him. His companionship had meant much to her, especially in times of crisis, such as when they had searched the Scriptures together when Carl Voight had so disturbed their minds. She had often thought of this difficult faith-shaking experience, and wondered what she would have done had it not been for the keen-minded, God-stabilized

Ares. She loved him deeply, and would miss him greatly. The war could not last much longer, she reasoned, and then would come a happy reunion.

Diamondola and her mother prepared gifts to send with Ares to the Keanides sisters in Greece. In this way, they could almost feel as if they had made personal contact with their loved ones.

The day of parting came. It was harder for Ares and Diamondola to be separated from each other than either had realized. Only confidence and trust in God's providences and leadership helped them to face it bravely.

Together Mother, Diamondola, and Ares went to the docks. They had taken many pleasant excursions together since their engagement almost a year before. But this last walk was different. Reluctantly they walked from the horse carriage, down the docks, and to the gangplank. The whistle blew, and Mother shook Ares' hand, then discreetly turned her back on the lovers.

Ares took Diamondola's small hand in his once more.

*The Thessalonica church members. Ares, Diamondola's fiancée, is in the back row, fourth from the left.*

"Diamondola," he said tenderly, "if God is willing, He will bring us together again. I hope it will be soon. Although you'll have both my work as well as yours to do in the office, please do not work beyond your strength. When I look at you, so fragile, so sweet, so perfect, I worry about your breaking under the strain. Please take good care of yourself. Someday soon, I hope, I'll be back, and then it won't be farewell, but hello, until death do us part."

"I know," she whispered, looking down with tear-filled eyes.

He gathered his little Diamondola into his strong arms, and held her close. Suddenly, the whistle blew again. The time of departure had come.

Ares wanted to leave her with happy memories of their parting, so he said almost cheerfully, "Practice well on my farewell gift to you. Have a happy song ready for me when I return."

He kissed her tenderly, and with a wave of his hand and a brave smile, he climbed the gangplank. Slowly the ship pulled out of the harbor, leaving Diamondola and her mother on the docks watching the ship sail down the Bosporus. Somehow she felt utterly alone.

Alone? No, never alone. God was always near her, and Mother stood by her side. But somehow she had a feeling that she might never again see Ares. She felt as though she had told him good-by forever. Not an eternal forever—just an earthly forever. Yet, even to say an earthly forever farewell to the man she loved was almost more than she could bear.

## CHAPTER XXII
# *Victories for God*

> *"But thanks be to God, which giveth us the victory through our Lord Jesus Christ" (l Cor. 15:57).*

Ares was gone, and his absence left a void no one else could fill. Diamondola was lonely, and felt she needed release from her worries. She decided to attend the motion-picture theater once a week, as she had when the Voights were still sharing her flat.

At first she seemed to enjoy seeing the motion pictures, but each week she gained less satisfaction from watching them. There seemed to be so little time and so much to do before Jesus came. Wasn't she wasting both time and money in such a place? Yet she seemed unable to break the habit. She finally came to the realization that she was addicted to the movies, and that movies were definitely a trap of the devil to lead her on to perdition. She prayed that the Lord would show her something to do that would not bring condemnation.

One night she left her mother to go to the theater. A strange excitement possessed her being. It is a good thing, she thought, that Mother, and Ares, and Elder Frauchiger don't know where I spend Sunday nights when I'm not translating for an evangelistic meeting. But then—and this thought made her stop dead in her tracks. God knew where she went. No one had ever told Diamondola that it was wrong to attend theaters, nevertheless she sensed that it was wrong. She knew that angels and Jesus would never spend their time looking at such frivolous things. The thought suddenly struck her: Why not spend her time and money helping the poor and sick each Sunday night? This seemed to be the answer to her prayer.

Diamondola turned away from the theater. With the small amount of money she had in her purse, she made her way toward the home of old Sister Hosanna. On the way, she bought some food. Sister Hosanna was most happy to see her, and she was deeply grateful for the food.

That night when Diamondola went home she could tell her mother with a clear conscience just how she had spent her time and her money. She knew that the record in heaven looked a whole lot better too. Every Sunday night after that, except when she was needed as a translator or gave Bible studies, Diamondola spent her time and money doing missionary work for the sick, the poor, or the aged. God had helped her to break her bad habit by substituting a good one in its place.

In April, 1915, the Allies landed at Gallipoli on the Dardanelles. This brought the war directly to Turkey. The war in Europe had kept the Allies more than occupied up to this time. With this new turn of events Turkey needed more money with which to buy equipment for the men in the army. Consequently, a conscript was permitted to buy his release. This money would in turn go to buy more and better equipment for those who did not wish, or were unable, to buy their release.

In May, Professor Tcharakian bought his way out of the army and returned to Constantinople. With him was his friend Aram Ashod, who also had bought his way out. Tcharakian requested baptism. Aram, however, looked upon all these joyous proceedings with serious doubts. Ashod and Tcharakian had been good friends. Ashod had led Tcharakian from atheism to a knowledge of the living God. As a result, he had joined Ashod's church. Now Ashod watched and listened with consternation as Tcharakian advanced beyond anything he had taught him. Tcharakian was joining a Sabbath keeping church, and of this Ashod plainly disapproved. He wondered whether the attractive little brunette translator had anything to do with it But though Ashod chided his friend a great deal, Tcharakian remained firm in his decision to be baptized into the Adventist Church.

A few weeks later there was great rejoicing in the little Adventist company of believers as Tcharakian, along with others, was united with the church in baptism. Even during troublous times the Lord was adding to His church. It encouraged the Turkish believers to see that the power of the gospel was so strong that it drew people from all walks of life.

If Diamondola and the church were happy that Tcharakian had been baptized, Ashod was not. He used all his arguments and influence to dissuade his friend from uniting with this obscure sect of Sabbath keepers, but in vain.

At last Ashod left his stubborn friend and went his way, saying, "I will go home and read the Bible through. I will write down all the texts I can find to prove that you are wrong in this new belief. Then I think you will listen to me instead of listening to Frauchiger and Diamondola."

"You fail to understand, my dear Aram," Tcharakian replied quietly, "that the Word of God in the hands of the simple and prudent as well as in the hands of the learned and educated is a most powerful tool. God's Spirit speaks through man to man."

"We shall see whether the Spirit will speak to me, or whether He is partial to Greeks and Germans and professors!" Ashod retorted.

## CHAPTER XXIII
# *Imprisoned for God*

*"But when they deliver you up, take no thought how or what ye shall speak: for it shall be given you in that same hour what ye shall speak"*
*(Matt. 10:19).*

Abdul-Hamid II took the Turkish throne in 1876. He proposed the policy of killing off the conquered races within his empire and promised reforms, which he did not carry out. In 1908 he was deposed by a reform party called the Young Turks. This group proclaimed a liberal program for the nation and demanded a constitutional government. But in a few years, they allowed Turkey to lapse into its old ways.

Hamid's old policy of genocide was put into effect in June and July of 1915. The German Allies recommended exile rather than outright murder of the victims, and the Turks were more than zealous in carrying out the suggestion.

When the government orders to deport Armenians arrived in a village, the local authorities rounded them up with ruthless alacrity. Most men between twenty and forty-five were drafted into the army, and the women and children were given twenty-four hours to prepare for exile. The cities along the Bosporus and the railroads were first evacuated. Later the barbarous orders were enlarged to include the whole of Turkey.

In June, the mission office was flooded with messages from the believers in the interior. Refugees who had managed to escape from the interior told gruesome stories of the fearful atrocities being perpetrated against the hapless Armenian Christians. It was felt that Elder Frauchiger and Diamondola should go immediately to the interior to see what they could do to help the members. After making the matter a subject of prayer, they decided to go to the interior with documents proving that the Adventist Armenians in no case had deserted to the enemy ranks. They hoped that they could establish that Adventists were loyal citizens, and Christians associated with a mission organization that had its headquarters in Germany. They hoped that the fact that the head of the Adventist mission in Turkey, Elder Frauchiger, was a German-speaking Swiss would help. By thus clarifying the Adventist position, Frauchiger and Diamondola hoped to relieve the suffering of the Adventist believers and save those who were still alive.

When they began to work on travel permits to visit the churches in the interior, they were hindered by obstacles on every hand. The German consul thought they were foolish to attempt such a journey.

The Turkish Government could scarcely be expected to be more helpful, since they had ordered the massacre of the Christians. However, after several weeks of persistent effort, Diamondola and Elder Frauchiger finally managed to get a promise that they would receive a travel permit.

This permit, promised on a Thursday, was to be called for at the police station the following Sabbath. The Sabbath School and church services that day followed the usual pattern, except that there was a special season of prayer. The members prayed that the believers in the interior would be delivered from their persecutors, and that Diamondola and Elder Frauchiger might have a successful journey. Some of the members put money in the hands of the missionaries to give to their afflicted brethren in the interior. When the farewells were said Elder Frauchiger and Diamondola started to the police station to pick up their travel papers. On the way to the streetcar, a secret military police officer fell in step with them.

Tapping Diamondola on the shoulder, he said quietly, "We want you at the police station. Follow me." Diamondola and Elder Frauchiger stared speechlessly at each other. Why would the police want them? She tried vainly to calm her fears by persuading herself that the summons had something to do with the travel papers.

As the three boarded the streetcar Diamondola felt weak. She and Elder Frauchiger seated themselves on the nearest empty seat, while the officer took one directly behind them.

"What do you want with us?" Diamondola asked the officer innocently, turning around. He glanced down at her, "Oh, just a few questions," he said casually, then added ominously, "It is you we wish to interrogate, not the gentleman with you."

Fear clutched her heart. What calamity was about to befall her? She knew that most "questionings" in those days led to conviction, and that women convicts preferred to face a firing squad than to endure the humiliations that usually accompanied imprisonment. War seemed to bring out the worst in men. The unfortunate victims of their passions were subjected to such inhumane handling that it would have made the men of Sodom blush with shame and plead for pity.

Diamondola sat on the streetcar dreading to reach the designated station. Her initial shock subsided, and she regained her composure, but she needed courage to face the crisis. She leaned over and explained her fear in German to Elder Frauchiger.

The fatherly man of God patted her hand gently and said, "Pray silently, Diamondola, and I'm going to stay right with you wherever they take you." This bit of comfort lifted her spirits, but her real strength came as she sent her silent petitions heavenward.

The three left the streetcar at the stop nearest the police station. The officer presented Diamondola to the police sergeant, who ordered her thrown into the dungeon with the lowest of criminals. Rough men wrenched her trembling hand from Elder Frauchiger's arm, and she was shoved down the dark, damp steps. A large key opened a squeaky, rusty door, and she was thrust into the darkness of the dungeon.

There on the floor of the dungeon she knelt, fear clutching at her heart.

"O Lord God," she gasped, "I trust Thee. Keep me safe." Peace flooded her throbbing breast and she relaxed against the wall. In the dense darkness, she could see nothing. Soon she heard the curses of the other unfortunates, and as her eyes gradually became accustomed to the darkness, she saw mingled on the dungeon floor fornicators, murderers, and robbers—sinners who had drunk their last cups of iniquity and were intoxicated with its dregs. They sneered at her, still dressed in her Sabbath clothes, as they argued with shameless immodesty who among them would be first to spoil her chastity.

Diamondola again turned to God for protection. She began to preach to those debased men and women about the love of God. She told them about the death of Jesus on the cross to save them from their sins. As she talked on about heaven and judgment, their sneers and curses gradually turned into tears of repentance. Several hours later when the guard appeared at the door he found the inmates of the dungeon much subdued. He summoned Diamondola, and she went with him to see the commissioner.

"You are to be court-martialed!" the commissioner announced in steel-crisp tones. "You are charged with sending reports to Rodosto [Tekirdag]."

Before the shock of this statement had had time to register, the commissioner dropped another bomb.

"You are summoned to appear before Bedri Bey. Take her away." With that, the heartless commissioner dismissed her case without a flicker of sympathy.

"Bedri Bey!" exclaimed Diamondola unbelievingly. Bedri Bey was the cruel chief of security for wartime Turkey. His name struck terror to the heart of all the inhabitants of the country. His ruthless ways of dealing with those who came under his power showed no mercy or justice. Diamondola realized that she was condemned already, for in Bedri Bey's world of justice an accusation was tantamount to condemnation—and that usually meant death by some means.

Diamondola protested that she knew no one in Rodosto. She had written no letters there. she wasn't even certain where Rodosto was. But all of her protestations of innocence were useless, and she was ushered unceremoniously out of the station toward the Office of Terror.

Outside the door Elder Frauchiger fell into step with Diamondola and her guard. Diamondola was happy to see him, but she knew that even his presence could not avert her fate.

On the way, she and Elder Frauchiger discussed what to do. They finally decided that Diamondola had better take a suitcase of clothing with her just in case her detention should be long. Somehow they persuaded the guard to escort them to Bedri Bey's office via Diamondola's home. The guard agreed, and waited at the bottom of the stairs while Diamondola hurried up the five flights to her apartment.

"It's about time you returned, darling." Mother greeted her daughter with a kiss and a worried expression. "I was afraid you were having trouble."

"Oh, yes, a bit, Mother," Diamondola replied as casually as possible.

She did not wish to worry Mother. Elder Frauchiger and Diamondola hoped that somehow God would deliver her in a few weeks from the clutches of prison and death. They felt that there was no need to disturb Mrs. Keanides yet. They had also agreed not to alarm the church members until such a time as it seemed absolutely necessary. The two would pretend they were going on a missionary journey to Rodosto. If worst came to worst, Elder Frauchiger would inform those concerned of Diamondola's fate. It was not a pleasant thought, but they felt that there was no need to raise any alarm unless it became absolutely necessary.

If Theodora detected anything unusual about Diamondola's silence, she did not indicate her concern in any way. She helped Diamondola pack her suitcase and prepared some food for her. She did wonder a bit about the sudden rush to be off on the missionary journey, but she realized that the members in the interior needed her help, and raised no further question.

With her suitcase hastily but thoughtfully packed, and a sandwich in her hand, Diamondola threw her arms around her mother and kissed her. Perhaps, she thought, it is the last time. Sobs rose in her throat, but she valiantly choked them back. Realizing that her strained emotions would soon pass beyond the point of control, she kissed her mother once more, grabbed her suitcase, and raced down the steps without looking back.

On the way to the Bedri Bey's security office, the three passed by several other police posts. Each time the guard had registered the fact that the terrible criminal Diamondola Keanides had reached that post without escaping. They chanced to pass through the police office that had their travel permit papers. There they were told contemptuously, "So you are the two spies who were going to the interior to stir up more of your mischief." To the espionage charge was now added the charge of sabotage. The future appeared hopeless.

When they finally reached Bedri Bey's office, they found that the chief was out. This was providential. His assistant informed them curtly that Diamondola must go at once to Rodosto to defend herself before the court there. Elder Frauchiger pleaded on her behalf, but the best he was able to do was to get a two-day postponement. Diamondola must go to Rodosto the following Monday. Elder Frauchiger was able to persuade the chief office assistant that he would be security for Diamondola if she were allowed to return with him to her home until Monday.

The two workers left the security office and went to the mission building. No one was there. However, they did learn that a church member who had seen Diamondola and Elder Frauchiger with a security policeman had reported his discovery to Mrs. Keanides and Mrs. Frauchiger.

From the mission office, the two workers walked to the Frauchiger apartment, arriving there at midnight. Inside the living room they found Diamondola's mother, almost frantic with fear, and other faithful church members gathered for prayer. A shout of praise rang out as the relieved members surrounded them. But their joy was short-lived, for Elder Frauchiger related the seriousness of their problem. Diamondola was really not free. Fear and despondency settled down once more on the group when they learned that Diamondola must go alone to Rodosto on Monday.

On Sunday night, a large group of believers gathered again in Frauchiger's home. They prayed most earnestly that God would intervene to save Diamondola from the trip to Rodosto. All of them knew that girls who went to prison became physical wrecks for the rest of their lives, even if they were released.

Some suggested that Diamondola hide; others suggested that she escape to Greece, where she could find refuge with Alexandra. A lawyer argued that if she could be declared physically ill, the government would delay her case fifteen days.

But Diamondola courageously insisted, "This is a time of severe trial to the body of the church as a whole. If I escape, it will compromise Elder Frauchiger's position, because he declared that he would be security for me. If I hide, I will surely be found, and my case will be more hopeless than it is at the present. The whole church will be under suspicion as collaborators against the cause of Turkish justice. We must not, through lack of faith and courage to die, imperil the position of the church—Christ's church. If it is God's will that my case be delayed until such time as I am better prepared to face the crisis, then I will become ill—genuinely ill."

After this speech of surrender and courage every eye was moist but every soul was strengthened. Elder Frauchiger agreed that Diamondola's suggestion was the only honest solution.

"And now," the elder said, "let us kneel for prayer."

Once more the assembled company knelt silently as Elder Frauchiger poured out his request to God. He prayed specifically that if it was God's will, Diamondola might become sick. After the Amen the supplicants waited silently for God's answer.

When they finally rose from prayer the room was hushed, and every eye was focused on Diamondola's face.

"Well, faith without works is dead," said Elder Frauchiger, breaking the silence. "Will someone please get the thermometer and take Diamondola's temperature?"

After three minutes, it was reported that Diamondola had a temperature of more than 102°. A government doctor was called and confirmed the findings. Just what was the cause of her sickness, he could not tell. But his report to the security office obtained a reprieve of fifteen days.

The next day, however, Diamondola was back at the office. Her temperature had left her almost as soon as the government doctor had gone. Now that she had a fifteen-day reprieve she must utilize every moment. If she should not return from Rodosto, Elder Frauchiger would be triply overtaxed with the work at the mission office. She caught up on the work, and even got ahead a bit on the next quarter's Sabbath School lessons. She did some soul searching as well, and when the fifteen days were over she felt better prepared, both physically and spiritually, to meet the crisis.

Four o'clock Monday morning arrived. A heavy fist thumping on the Frauchiger's door made everyone shudder as they realized that the police had come for Diamondola. The last good-byes were said, the last embraces loosened, but the last tears had not yet been shed. The Adventist brethren watched as the gendarme led Diamondola away alone. As the first streaks of dawn appeared in the east a pall of gloom rested upon the believers' hearts. It seemed as if they were watching Diamondola's funeral—as if she were walking into her grave.

Diamondola was led from one police station to another until at last she reached the central office. It was eight o'clock by then, and the hardhearted officer in charge ruled that it was too late to send the prisoner to Rodosto that day. So, she was sent to the "guest house." Diamondola knew that the "guest house" was the place where condemned victims were held until they were hanged in the gallows chamber.

Diamondola shuddered as she entered the courtyard of the building that sealed the doom for many innocent, as well as guilty, persons. She was detained in a court holding fifteen other women prisoners—members of the lowest dregs of society. They greeted her with blasphemous language and coarse jests. Diamondola silently and unobtrusively found a place on the floor near the edge of the group, and offered a silent prayer. Then, remaining with head bowed, she waited for an answer as Tcharakian always did. Suddenly she felt impressed that God had a work for her to do right there among these degenerates. She opened her Turkish Bible and read aloud from the Psalms. The effect was dramatic. Once more Diamondola was able to bring light and encouragement to prisoners doubly bound—bound by literal chains and by the fetters of sin. She prayed individually for each handcuffed sufferer, and the whole group retired to their individual mats feeling happier than they had felt in months. Their burdens had been lifted as light pierced through their sin-darkened souls, giving them new insight and hope.

The next morning the hardened keeper of the "guest house" released Diamondola to her special guard, declaring, "I have never seen such a girl. She is not human—she is an angel. In a few hours, her presence wrought a miracle among these women. My wife and I have never seen a prisoner like her. She cannot be guilty of any crime. I wish I could personally secure her release. She is an angel, I tell you!"

It was well for Diamondola that she had sewed a row of gold coins in her belt. She soon needed them. When she and her gendarme set out the next morning, she discovered that she was expected to pay the train fare. When they arrived at the Rodosto station, she had to bargain for a carriage to drive them to the town three hours' distant by road. Fearful of making this trip with only her rough soldier as escort, she begged an Armenian woman and her daughter, who also were bound for Rodosto, to share the carriage. But they refused, fearing that they would get involved in her trouble. Alone in the carriage with the gendarme, Diamondola soon became conscious of his bold stares. She needed protection! Again, she thought of the protection that is better than sword or gun—God and His Word. She opened her Bible and diverted the interest of her Moslem escort from herself to the prophecies of Daniel. He was intrigued by the study of the rise and fall of nations so accurately fulfilled by the passing of time. He was immensely impressed with her religion and her character.

When they reached Rodosto, the gendarme refused to let Diamondola send a telegram of safe arrival to her mother, assuring her positively that any young woman with such high standards and good character would soon be set free—that she would probably reach home before the telegram did. Diamondola wished that she felt as confident as he did.

Inside the courtroom they were told that Diamondola's case could not be heard until the next day. The gendarme whispered something in the officer's ear, who in turn whispered something to someone else. Soon the gendarme had permission for Diamondola to spend the night in a hotel instead of the prison. Here, as with the carriage, she was expected to pay for his board and room as well as her own.

The next morning her trial was held. She was arraigned before five austere judges, who sat on one side of a table facing her. She faced her judges calmly, for had she not the assurance, "And ye shall be brought before governors and kings for my sake, for a testimony against them and the Gentiles. But when they deliver you up, take no thought how or what ye shall speak: for it shall be given you in that same hour what ye shall speak. For it is not ye that speak, but the Spirit of your Father which speaketh in you" (Matt. 10:18–20).

Diamondola was resigned to life or death, imprisonment or deliverance. She rested her confidence in God's promise. She realized that she was unaware of reasons for the charges brought against her. However, she did know that she was charged with circulating reports and was up for court-martial. She only knew she trusted God. He would give her the words that she should speak. The scene in that courtroom in Rodosto looked awesome. Five solemn judges seated behind a table to question one small girl standing before them. Yet, had their eyes been opened, the police, the judges, and the spectators would have beheld legions of angels hovering near God's humble little servant.

The central figure at the judge's table began the questioning. In a stern voice intended to strike fear into the prisoner he asked, "Diamondola Keanides, are you employed by an organization that calls itself the Levant Union Mission?"

"Yes, sir," she answered directly, without the slightest tremor in her voice.

"Is it your job to circulate letters and propaganda for them?"

"I am the secretary for that Protestant church organization. The headquarters for our church is in Germany. When certain lessons on the Bible come from Germany, I translate them and send them to our church members throughout Turkey. I also write letters to some of the members and workers. I do not call any of my work propaganda, sir."

"I call it propaganda, and I have proof," he shouted, raising his voice to such intensity that the roof almost shook.

Diamondola had no intention of competing with the volume of the judge's voice, and remained quiet.

The judge brought out the "proof." It was the letter that Diamondola had sent to Professor Tcharakian six months before. Tcharakian had kept the letter in his valise. When he had moved from one barracks to another, his brief case had been stolen by the Turkish porter. Diamondola suddenly caught the connection. What the judges did not know was that the porter, eager to gain some money and recognition, had evidently turned over the written and printed material to the authorities. What the illiterate porter did not know, and what the authorities had overlooked, was that all the literature had previously been approved by the government. The only piece that gave the least cause for suspicion was one sentence in one of her handwritten letters. As the "evidence" was handed to her she saw two, and only two, sentences underscored in red. They read: "Last Sabbath Brother Baharian preached a very influential sermon. You would have liked to have heard it."

"How do you account for that sentence in your letter? What does it mean? What would Baharian, an Armenian, speak about that could be so influential? Are you and Baharian and Tcharakian and a host of others members of some secret organization working under the guise of religion?"

And the judges waxed eloquent as they went on and on in their accusations and condemnations. But the burden of each speech was the same: Diamondola, a Greek Christian, was the secretary-treasurer of a new secret society that was plotting against the government, and that the sentence in her letter inferred much more than it actually stated. Her life was at stake as a traitor. The future looked dark and hopeless.

When she was first arrested and accused, she had been shocked and desperately fearful; but the day of her trial found her calm and confident. She had made her peace with God and was ready for whatever came. While looking directly and serenely at the judges, she offered a silent prayer to her Advocate, who had promised to tell her what she should speak in this hour. He did not fail her.

"Honorable judges," she began quietly but firmly, "before answering your questions, it is necessary for me to show you what kind of person I am, and what my people represent, what we believe, and what we teach.

But I cannot do so without a book that I have, which is in my suitcase at the hotel."

To her surprise and relief, the gendarme was dispatched to fetch her suitcase. In a few minutes she took from it a Turkish-Greek Bible for her personal use and a Turkish Bible, which she opened and handed to the chief judge, so that he could follow what she was reading. She then gave an exposition based on three theses: (1) The Christian's duty toward his government as interpreted by Paul in the thirteenth chapter of Romans. (2) The Christian's duty toward his God and His laws as given in Exodus twenty, elaborating on the second commandment, which condemns the use of idols in any form—a custom abhorrent to the Moslems and emphasizing that the Seventh-day Adventists detest idol worship as much as do Moslems. (3) The Christian's duty toward himself, with reference to the distinction between clean and unclean meats, as described in the eleventh chapter of Leviticus. On this point Diamondola explained emphatically that Seventh-day Adventists scrupulously refrain from using tobacco, alcohol, and pork. This latter point greatly impressed her Moslem judges. For two hours Diamondola, under the influence of God's Spirit, delivered a powerful sermon to her judges. The hush that fell upon the courtroom during those two hours could be described as almost reverent. The judges themselves appeared as if they were being arraigned before the judgment bar of God, and they trembled as they were convicted of their sins and unworthiness.

When Diamondola finished, the judges allowed her to be seated while they reached their decision—an unusual concession. As her fate trembled in the balance, she knew she had done her best to represent the Adventist cause aright. She rested her case in God's hands, believing that He would help her, and that, whatever their decision, her judges had heard a message from God.

While the judges discussed her case, she waited quietly. She closed her Bible and replaced it in her valise. Paul, she thought, had almost persuaded his royal listeners to become Christians, and yet, convinced as they were of the truth, they had refused to acquit him. She was not as worthy as Paul, and was resigned to whatever decision the judges would reach. Presently she became aware that everything was quiet. Looking up, still calm and serene, she found the chief judge looking benevolently down into her face.

"My dear girl," he began with words reflecting a kindness quite unnatural for a military judge of any nation, "we are sorry we have troubled you so much. Almost you have persuaded us to be like you. We Moslems abhor many of the same things you preach against, but we do not always practice what is right as faithfully as you do. Seventh-day Adventists are better Moslems than we are. We are happy to find in our land people who live out the principles of our religion. We can see now that you Adventists are loyal citizens of our country and are devoted servants of Allah. May Allah be merciful to you always. You are acquitted. Go in peace. By the way," he added as an afterthought, "Rodosto is famous for its delicious watermelons. Take one to your mother."

The sudden turn of events left Diamondola speechless. Resigned to being condemned, she couldn't believe she had been acquitted. She stood stock-still, her eyes fixed on the smiling judge.

"Come on!" prompted her gendarme, prodding her gently.

"Oh, thank you, honorable judges," she managed to say at last. Then bowing respectfully, she stumbled out of the courtroom exuberant with joy. She was free!

Off again they went, Diamondola and her gendarme. First by carriage and then by rail. How different the road looked now! The same road that had seemed haunted with danger and dark forebodings, now seemed lighted with peace and freedom. She was going home. Home! The word had never sounded so good to her.

It was late at night when the train neared Constantinople. The gendarme, whom his prisoner had treated as a guest, dropped off at a station near his home, and left her to complete the journey alone. At the big station in the city Diamondola tried in vain to find a carriage to take her home. Great convoys of wounded men had come in from the Dardanelles and all carriages had been commandeered for army use. Diamondola lived on the other side of the city. It was night, and it would take her nearly an hour to walk home. There seemed to be no other alternative but to take her chances and trust in God. With her valise in hand, and her heart pounding with joyful anticipation of the great reunion she and Mother would have, she bounded off down the street.

As Diamondola was wending her way home, a disheartened group of Christians were gathered in her home praying for her. The scene was reminiscent of the prayer meeting that took place in Jerusalem nineteen centuries before on behalf of the apostle Peter, who was in prison awaiting execution. It was now three days since Diamondola had been taken, and the telegram she had promised to send from Rodosto had not been received. They concluded that she had not reached Rodosto, but had met her fate in the "guest house." The brethren were comforting Theodora with the promise of a reunion on the resurrection day. But one man present kept shaking his head.

"Wait on the Lord, I say," said Elder Frauchiger, "wait. Why do you doubt? Why are you discouraged and defeated? Where is the God of Peter, who delivered him from prison? Where is the God of Daniel, who delivered him from the lions' den? Where is the God of the Hebrews, who saved them from a most certain death in the fiery furnace? Is Diamondola's God not the same God of those servants of old? He is the same yesterday, today, and forever. God is with her. I tell you, brethren, if He is willing, He is able to deliver her from the Turkish military courts! I will wait and see His salvation."

The room was hushed as new courage filled their hearts.

The group knelt once more as Elder Frauchiger suggested, "Let us pray."

There was a gentle knock at the door.

Elder Frauchiger's voice trembled with praise, "O we thank Thee, God, for answering our prayers and bringing Diamondola back safely to us. Amen."

Another knock, a bit louder this time, accompanied by an excited voice calling, "Mother! Mother!"

Elder Frauchiger opened the door and Diamondola walked in.

God had answered their prayers.

CHAPTER XXIV
# *The Second Attempt*

*"And they were scattered, because there is no shepherd:
and they became meat to all the beasts of the field, when they were scattered.
My sheep wandered through all the mountains, and upon every high hill:
yea, my flock was scattered upon all the face of the earth, and none did
search or seek after them" (Ezek. 34:5, 6).*

After only a day's rest Diamondola was back again at work in the office. It was the end of July, and time to pay the workers. On her pay roll that month was a new worker-Diran Tcharakian. He had left his work at the university and joined the ministerial force of the Levant Union Mission. As Diamondola handed him his paycheck, he accepted it gratefully, even though it was twenty times less than what he had received as a professor at the university. Tcharakian lived a life of dedicated service to his Master. He was ever a faithful, loving, willing, and humble servant, who never complained no matter what his lot might be. No task was too menial or inconsequential for Tcharakian. He became the "new apostle"—a fitting example of what a servant of God should be. If Diamondola was ever discouraged from overwork, or the fact that mail had stopped coming through from Ares and her sisters, she thought of Tcharakian. His wife had left him; his friends shunned him; his fellow professors at the university considered him crazy; and even his trusted friend, Ashod, was no longer on speaking terms with him. Yet Tcharakian was so thankful for the knowledge of the truth and the privilege of serving God that it made Diamondola ashamed that she had ever allowed herself to become discouraged.

Late that summer Diamondola and Elder Frauchiger received an invitation from the Greek Orthodox patriarch asking for Bible studies on the book of Revelation. The patriarch was writing a study on the Apocalypse, because he felt that Revelation contained a message for his day, but he was having difficulty in understanding certain passages. He had heard that Seventh-day Adventists were students of the Bible and its prophecies, so he telephoned Elder Frauchiger to secure his services.

"Please come and study with us every Thursday morning at ten o'clock," he urged. "After the study we will have dinner together with my vestrymen in the parish house."

In response to this request Diamondola and Elder Frauchiger studied the book of Revelation for some time with the patriarch. He had much to unlearn and many prejudices to overcome, but he made remarkable advances. Because his vestrymen were not the scholars that their revered patriarch was, they followed along more slowly, and at times almost halted the progress of the studies. At such times, Elder Frauchiger, with Diamondola translating, explained the particular passage more fully. Meanwhile the patriarch, sitting at the opposite end of the table, and surrounded by reference books, writing materials, and his Bible, filled the margins of his papers with additional notes. When the lesson was completed, the study group, consisting of ten to twelve members of the Greek Orthodox patriarchate, was led in prayer by the teachers, after which all rose from the table. The table was then quickly and efficiently cleared by the servants. A snowy white damask tablecloth was spread over the polished veneer, and dainty chinaware and fine tableware were placed quickly on the table by skilled hands. In only a matter of minutes Diamondola and Elder Frauchiger joined the patriarch and his vestrymen in what was the Adventist guests' best meal of the week. This procedure continued until the book of Revelation was completed.

The flock of God in the central eastern section of Turkey were being scattered throughout the hills and mountains. Elder Frauchiger and

Diamondola had attempted to seek after them, and help them, but their plans had to be abandoned when Diamondola had been arrested.

Meanwhile a secret message was received at the mission office that there was special trouble brewing for the Christians in Iconium. Ares' mother arrived one day at the mission headquarters and verified the rumor. She also disclosed the information that she had received word from Ares to the effect that he would like her to join him in Greece for the duration of the war. The mission advanced the travel money, and she went to Greece. Before she left, Diamondola gave her a letter and a special gift for Ares. Diamondola longed to accompany her, but her work would not permit it. How she missed Ares, not only because of his help in the office but because of his companionship as well. Since it was impossible for her to be with Ares, it was good that she had a busy church and office program, for it kept her from thinking too much about her loneliness. One day Tcharakian came bounding into the office with a joyful expression on his face, tears brimming in his deep brown eyes.

"Oh," he exclaimed thankfully to Diamondola, 'I'm so happy. Ashod, my dear friend, is converted. I've prayed so much for him. I couldn't communicate with him personally since last May when he became angry with me for becoming an Adventist. But I asked God to send the Holy Spirit to speak to him, and he began reading the Bible through in order to prove to me how wrong I have been about the law and the Sabbath. When he got to Psalm 119 he broke down. That chapter speaks about the law in almost every verse. He said that the Spirit of God convicted him so strongly of the importance of the law that he simply destroyed all the notes that he thought were evidence against Sabbath keeping. He is not fully converted yet, but I believe he will go all the way with God—and soon. Oh, Diamondola, with God as my partner I can never fail. His Spirit works when I can't, and souls are converted. I am praying Ashod will be in church next Sabbath."

And Ashod was in church the next Sabbath. Diamondola noticed the young man on the back seat listening attentively to her translation of Elder Frauchiger's sermon. Ashod was on the back seat the following Sabbath, and many Sabbaths thereafter. But one thing puzzled her, Ashod always slipped out the back door as soon as the benediction was said. Elder Frauchiger and Diamondola were never given a chance to shake hands with him or to speak with him as they did the other members. If Tcharakian had been there she felt that he could have persuaded Ashod to stay around longer after the service. But Tcharakian was a missionary in his own right and was busy among the villages of western Turkey, preaching the gospel with great success wherever he went. The service he rendered was unique. As a university professor, he could reach the elite, yet his simplicity endeared him to the common man. His sermons were as influential as his prayers were powerful.

The Adventist membership in and around Constantinople was increasing, but from the interior came reports that the members were being decimated by persecution. As a good shepherd of the Lord's flock, Elder Frauchiger was continually thinking about the suffering ones. "Diamondola," he announced solemnly one morning, "we must make a missionary journey to the interior and try to find and help our dear brethren and sisters. I cannot bear to think of their suffering while we make no attempt to help them."

"But," Paul Bridde pointed out, "you did try to help them once. The German consul thought you were crazy for trying, and Diamondola was imprisoned. Have you forgotten that experience so soon?"

"No, I haven't forgotten," Elder Frauchiger answered, as a look of pain crossed his face, "but neither have I forgotten those dear souls in the interior. Some have already died on the death march into the Syrian Desert. Others will no doubt be taken soon. I must go and see if I can find our people, rescue them if possible, and help them. If this is impossible, I must take money and clothing to those perishing along the way, and Diamondola must go with me." Then with tears in his eyes this godly man bowed his head on his arms.

During the next few weeks the church members collected blankets and warm clothing. The wealthier members contributed gold coins. Theodora practically cleaned out their closet, and some of their food money was turned into gold coins. Mrs. Frauchiger and Theodora sewed gold coins into the belts and vests of the two missionaries.

Elder Frauchiger and Diamondola set out upon their mission just before Christmas. They took with them bundles and suitcases and burlap bags full of clothing, and wore their gold-coin belts and vests. This time they secured travel permits, but every official they had to interview told them they were crazy. The German consul was angry. "All right, go, Frauchiger," he shouted, "but don't expect any pity if you and your secretary are deported along with the exiles!"

This was no idle threat, and the two travelers well knew that their mission was a perilous undertaking. Nevertheless, they decided to go. Diamondola had always done what the mission had asked her to do. She felt that a call from the mission to do a task was a call from God. Her father had always said, "God's biddings are enablings." She had learned to obey God's call and accept the consequences without complaint.

Many of the members gathered at the railway station and waved the missionaries a tearful good-by, but Theodora bravely blew Diamondola a last kiss as the train pulled out of the station. She believed that this second attempt to help the scattered flock was God's will, and that if Diamondola and Elder Frauchiger lost their lives in the attempt they would be perishing in line of duty.

## CHAPTER XXV
## *Where He Leads*

*"Even there shall thy hand lead me,
and thy right hand shall hold me" (Ps. 139:10).*

The first stop of the mercy mission was at Eskishehir. A lump arose in Diamondola's throat as the train approached the city of her birth. All her relatives had disowned her family when they became Protestants. They had not even been invited to Uncle Stephanos' wedding the fall before they had left Eskishehir. The Keanides had tried to correspond with Uncle Stephanos, for he was Mother's only living brother, but he replied only once. When Theodora wrote him that she had been baptized into the Adventist Church, he replied in a sarcastic vein, remarking about "unstable drifters, who go from one crazy sect into another more deplorable than the first." Father had once received a similar letter from his brother Elisha. "Mind you," it said, "those daughters of yours will never find a respectable husband now. I was so glad to hear that your sensible Susanna chose a man from her forefathers' church and settled down before you folks got caught up in this latest craze.

"P.S. Please let us know when you come to your senses, for we would like to see you again." This was the last the Keanides had heard from

Stephanos or Elisha. Now Diamondola found herself in Eskishehir. Since she had been only two and a half years old when she and her parents had moved away, she naturally did not remember the city at all. Since then father had died, and many of their relatives in Eskishehir had died, but she had the addresses of Uncle Elisha and Uncle Stephanos and cousin Sava. She had promised her mother to try to contact them all and witness her faith before them tactfully if an opportunity presented itself. Mother knew how bitterly opposed they were to Adventism, but she prayed daily for their conversion. She knew how sincere a person could be in his opposition to truth, for she had been a firm opposer for years.

"Maybe God is sending you to Eskishehir at this time, Diamondola," Theodora had said hopefully, "because now that persecution has come our relatives will be ready to listen."

When Elder Frauchiger and Diamondola got off the train, it took quite a bit of shuffling around to get all their baggage off. They shivered in the cold, icy air of the plateau city. Hiring a carriage, they drove to cousin Sava's house. Theodora had suggested that they go there, since he had shown many signs of friendliness the past few years, and by staying at his place they might be able to save those precious gold coins for the use of the suffering church members.

"Yes," Elder Frauchiger had agreed, "we must travel as inexpensively as possible so that more money can be made available to our suffering brethren."

When they reached cousin Sava's house he welcomed them with open arms. Diamondola was wearing her mother's hand-knit woolen stockings—quite inappropriate for sophisticated city wear, but most comfortable on the freezing plateau. She wore her vest of gold coins, her belt with more gold coins, and a heavy woolen dress, plus a sweater and a heavy coat. But nothing seemed to keep out the penetrating cold. She noted that Elder Frauchiger was also shivering. Cousin Sava seated them around a charcoal fire brazier. But they never really felt warm until they had eaten a bowl of hot potato and onion soup.

The next day they called at the homes of the church members. Diamondola had the complete list with addresses in her notebook. Some of the Adventist homes were completely deserted and ransacked. She knew that these Adventists had already been exiled. Other homes farther from the railway center were still intact and their occupants safe. These members had not yet been exiled and were not actually suffering. It was those who had been taken who were suffering. The route of deportation of the Christians was well known by the members of the interior, so Elder Frauchiger and Diamondola decided to follow the line and try to catch up with them to give them help and courage. But first, they would stay with the members in Eskishehir. The Armenian members who remained in Eskishehir knew that their fate hung precariously in the balance. They knew that at any time they could be exiled. These members were thrilled to see the office workers from the church's headquarters. They too needed encouragement for the crisis. Whole sections of the Armenian Christian quarters lay desolate. The Adventists had been taken indiscriminately with the rest.

"Just think, Diamondola," Elder Frauchiger had said as his eyes filled with tears, "only a few months ago those houses were filled with happy, carefree children, busy wives and mothers, and devoted fathers and husbands. Where are they all today? and how is it with them? O God, come quickly and rid us of this curse and misery."

Diamondola was moved with such pity at the tragedy around her. But worse sights were yet ahead.

One day Diamondola went with Sava to Uncle Stephanos' house. How would he feel toward her, she wondered. Uncle Stephanos greeted Sava warmly but eyed the strange girl questioningly. "You can't guess who this young lady is, can you?" asked Sava, eager to spring a surprise.

"Uh-no, —but there is something familiar about her." Uncle Stephanos paused, studying her features closely. "Her large brown eyes remind me of someone dear to me—but I don't recall ever having seen her before."

"Yes, you have. You were there the night she was named Little Diamond," explained Sava gleefully.

"Little Diamond? Why, can it be ..." Uncle Stephanos hesitated. "Can it be Diamondola?"

Diamondola smiled and nodded her head affirmatively. No longer hesitating, Uncle Stephanos clasped her in his strong arms. He was thrilled to see his niece, and she was thrilled by this sign of acceptance by her uncle whom she did not remember seeing before. Diamondola spent some time with Uncle Stephanos and told him all the latest news about the family. She also learned many details of interest to take back to Mother.

Sometime later that day she met Uncle Elisha, Father's brother. He also welcomed his brother's daughter. But neither of them was receptive to the Advent message. She was accepted, but her message was not, and this grieved the young missionary. But she hoped that the initial prejudices of her uncles had been broken down by her visit and that they would later come to believe as she did.

Upon the suggestion of cousin Sava, the missionary pair made their headquarters in his home. Sava was a Greek and was exempt from the Armenian deportations. Cousin Sava even invited them to hold meetings in his home, and his invitation was accepted.

The meetings turned out to be both revival and evangelistic in nature. Many non-Adventist neighbors and friends joined the Adventists in their services. The meeting room was crowded, in fact packed, and the group took turns sitting near the little brazier filled with charcoal.

One evening the people were so eager to listen to the Bible lectures that they gathered much earlier than expected. Cousin Sava had no time to properly prepare the charcoal fire. As a result, the charcoal gave off poisonous but odorless fumes. As Diamondola stood over the brazier, she inhaled these dangerous gases. Elder Frauchiger, standing just a bit behind her, didn't get the full force of the gas as she did. Before long Diamondola felt ill.

"Elder Frauchiger," she whispered in German, I'm terribly sick, I have a headache—a terrible headache—I can't go on."

"You must," he urged, "we cannot stop a meeting right now when the room is full of listeners. We can't disappoint these dear people."

"But I can't go on ... I ..." and with that Diamondola slumped over backward. Fortunately, the room was so packed that Elder Frauchiger, standing almost directly behind her, caught her and carried her out into the fresh air. Because of the sudden exertion, he nearly fainted too. He was getting sick without realizing it. The meeting was postponed until the speaker and translator recovered sufficiently to continue. Strange as it may seem, the people were so eager to hear the message that they all stayed on until the end of the sermon.

The meetings were successful. Some reconsecrated their lives to God and others were converted and became Adventists. A baptism could be held later, but now the missionaries had to move on and find the scattered flock dying from hunger and cold on the exile trail.

Diamondola and Elder Frauchiger stopped next at Aksehir. Here they visited the deportees' camp. Among the campers they found some of the Adventists from various towns to the west. The deportees were living in abject misery. All were cold and hungry, and many were sick and dying. One of the churchmen had lost his wife along the way. When he saw Diamondola crawl into his shelter to talk to him, he was overcome with emotion and grief. Squatting in his shelter, he rocked back and forth saying, "I have lost my wife. Poor dear, oh, poor dear. Though she was expecting, she was forced to walk fast with the rest of us. I lingered behind with her. She was so tired. The soldiers beat us because we were slowing down the crowd. They pushed her, and she fell in the snow. I was weak from hunger and could not carry her. Then her child was born prematurely there on the roadside, and he died. My wife, lacking proper medical care, and unable to walk, fell exhausted by the road. I stayed with her until-until-she passed away. She died because—well, I think she really wanted to. She had suffered so much, she bled so much, she was beaten so much, and she froze so much. I left her there in the snow lying in a pool of blood beside our infant son, who lived only a few minutes in the severe mountain cold. Oh, where is God? Why does He not care for us His children?" The man's wasted body shook with sobs.

Elder Frauchiger crawled under the shelter with the heartbroken brother. "My brother," he asked kindly, "was your wife a faithful servant of God?"

"Oh, yes, very faithful. She was an angel, and she loved God very much," the man replied with certainty through his sobs.

"Was she ready to die?" asked the missionary.

"I'm sure she was. In her dying breath, she prayed for the rough soldier who had pushed her into the snow, causing her such pain and misery and the death of our child," the brother added.

"Remember the verse in the Bible that says, 'All that will live godly in Christ Jesus shall suffer persecution.' She suffered unto death, but if she was ready, then she is spared the future possibility of falling into sin through other influences. I believe God took her life when she was ready, and your innocent son as well. Fear not, my brother, you will meet her again if you can remain faithful and forgiving. These soldiers are hardened through sin and ignorance of the gospel. They feel wearied in carrying out these orders, and they have become calloused to suffering, death, and misery. They do not regard the sacredness of life. They take life and cause suffering because they fear not God. These soldiers are the ones to be pitied. Their hearts are not receptive to God's Spirit, and their miserable, heartless life here will bring little joy to them. Think of the record they must face in the judgment. Would you care to exchange places with them, my brother?"

The man by now had regained his self-control and listened to Elder Frauchiger's reasoning.

"Oh, no, sir," he replied, "I'd rather be a deportee, ready to face my own record."

"Would you have wanted your poor wife to live longer and suffer more, that she might in the end have embittered her spirit against the injustices done to her?"

"No, I can't say that I would."

"Then," said Elder Frauchiger, softly laying his hand on the man's bony arm, "let us thank God that His will was done, for we would not choose to be led any way other than that which God leads us, if we could but see the end from the beginning, and discern the gloriousness of His purpose for us."

The man nodded silently. He accepted his lot. His bitterness toward God and man dissolved, and the light of forgiveness radiated from his emaciated face.

"Let us pray," said Elder Frauchiger, and the three bowed their heads in prayer.

"Now let us go and drink a bowl of hot soup. Diamondola and I bought some vegetables, and a big kettle of hot soup is being cooked for everyone."

Elder Frauchiger and Diamondola spent the next few days comforting the members, bringing them food, and giving them warm clothing. A few gold coins were taken from the missionaries' vests and belts, and sewed to each member's vest or belt.

The condition of the refugees was pathetic. They were huddled together under crude shelters that could not keep out the dampness and cold. They were usually banded in groups of eight or ten just enough for one gendarme to escort safely. The gendarmes had learned that if there were too many porters for one guard there was danger that the men might overpower him. So the groups were kept small. When a number of the deportees died, the survivors were regrouped, and the gendarmes who were not needed were sent home.

As the deportation bands moved along, Diamondola and Elder Frauchiger moved along with them. At Karahisar they found no members at all. All had been deported. To their knowledge not one Christian was left in the village.

Their next stop was Iconium. In Aksehir, Diamondola and Elder Frauchiger had slept under the crude shelters with the members, but in Iconium they rented rooms in a cheap hotel and stayed there at nights. Early each morning they went to the markets and purchased food that could easily be cooked over fires in tins or whatever vessels were available. The Adventist deportees fared a bit better because of the few days they were allowed to remain and rest at Iconium. But the deportees were never allowed to stay long in one place.

In Iconium the weather turned bitterly cold, so cold that Diamondola found it painful to breathe. Each morning the walk to the deportee camp was a trying experience. Although she was clad in the warmest clothing, she still shivered from the penetrating cold. As she and Elder Frauchiger arrived at the camp their hearts were wrung to see the miserable condition of their brethren. Diamondola longed to set them free and return them to their comfortable homes, shops, and farms. She knew many of them personally from the first missionary journey she had taken with Elder AcMoody back in 1907. Eight years had brought many changes, some of them good. But this sudden disruption of their homes and lives was not welcomed by any of them. Whole families were uprooted, grouped in gangs, and sent into exile. The roadside of the deportation route was littered with the bodies of the weak, the sick, or those who had been severely beaten or shot. The gendarmes never allowed relatives time to bury those who fell by the roadside. Often a sick one had to be left to die alone, and as the survivors looked back over the road, they could see the vultures circling the spot where the loved one had been left behind.

One man, grieving at the sight of the circling vultures that were waiting to devour his dying son, collapsed in anguish. The gendarme in charge of his group dismounted and beat the man with the butt of his gun.

"Hurry, you infidel," he yelled, "let's get to the next village before night. I want to carouse some tonight. Get up, you devil," he screamed with bestial passion.

But the man could not rise. So the infuriated gendarme beat the man's face to pulp with his rifle butt, and then kicked his body into the ditch. All this time the man's wife and daughter watched helplessly. The gendarme then mounted his horse and lashed at his group with his whip in order to force them to catch up with the other deportees.

Stirred by inhuman passions, he yelled, "Move along, you infidels, or I'll rid myself of the whole lot of you right now. The sooner I have finished my duty, the sooner I can return home. And," he sneered heartlessly, "my superior officers don't care whether you reach the Syrian Desert or not—just so you don't escape."

These were the stories of misery and suffering that Elder Frauchiger and Diamondola heard all day long while in Iconium. They knew very well that many with whom they spoke in Iconium would never make it to the next big stop, Eregli. The deportees pleaded for the workers to save them—to send them by train to Constantinople. Gladly would the workers have done this, but the Turkish Government officials would not consent. Once one was put into the deportee mass it was impossible to get out, except by death or an infrequent escape.

One man who escaped bribed his gendarme with a gold pound. The man's feet were swollen twice their normal size from the cold, so that he could no longer wear shoes. He removed his wool vest and tore it into rags and wrapped his feet in them. Finally, when he could endure the journey no longer he dug a hole in the snow, and gave his gendarme a gold pound to leave him alone to die in peace. The gendarme accepted the bribe, turned his back, and left the man to die. After his group had gone on, this man hobbled into the nearest village, where kind Moslem Turks cared for him in the name of God. Traveling by night, he made his way back to Iconium, and the French nuns' school. Here he found his sisters. His father and mother had died on the roadside. Later they moved with the Protestant school to Beirut, where he became an Adventist.

The day the exiles were leaving Iconium on their death march into the desert, Diamondola was confronted by a gendarme who told her to march with his group.

"But why must I be deported? I am a Greek from Constantinople," she objected.

"Well, we've seen you among the deportees and you speak Armenian well enough. We know you are one, too. So get along, you infidel," he shouted, giving her a rough shove toward the woeful deportees.

At this point Elder Frauchiger intervened. "Now, look," he said firmly, "you can't take this young girl. I am a German-Swiss, and she is my translator. She is a Greek and has learned to speak many languages, which is the reason she is employed for my work."

After uttering many unprintable curses the guard finally shouted, "—and get out of here yourself, you old disreputable father of the Christian pigs, or we'll take you too." It was no secret how he felt toward the missionaries, nor was there any question about how he felt toward his charges. He hated them intensely, and would gleefully have cut them to pieces.

"I'd drink all of their blood, if it wouldn't contaminate me," he declared.

Now Diamondola had been added to the long line of exiles. The guards were unreasonable, and insisted that though she was a Greek she was a Christian pig and an infidel. And since she was a Turkish citizen they could do with her as they wished, and there was nothing she could do about it. Elder Frauchiger was ungraciously invited to mind his own business.

Remembering he had some official-looking mission papers with him, he sought out the highest men in authority among the gendarmes, as well as among the city officials of Iconium, and after several hours of persuasive discussion, finally secured Diamondola's release.

The next and last stop on the way south and east was Eregli. Some deportees were allowed to ride the train and/or hire carriages to this place if they could afford it. But from Eregli into the desert the journey was to be made entirely on foot. The guards, of course, rode horses.

After Diamondola's narrow escape in Iconium it may have seemed unwise to pursue the exile trail farther, but she and Elder Frauchiger felt that they must try to alleviate the misery of the deportees as much as possible. They fully realized that they might be forced to join the exiles, but they were willing to take the risk. They had purposed in their hearts to do all they could to help, and if this meant exile, they were prepared to accept death along with the rest.

At each stop they had tried to get the Adventist deportees released, but it was hopeless. Protestants and Catholics suffered alike, just so long as they were Armenian Christians. It would have taken a special court investigation of each case to obtain freedom, and even then an acquittal would have depended upon the whim of the judge and the way the case was presented.

In Eregli the missionaries found the exiles in worse condition than at any previous stop. They found the members packed into an abandoned inn, along with some of the other refugees. To see human beings trying to survive in that broken-down structure made Diamondola weep. The suffering, sickness, and malnutrition that she saw among the campers beggars description. There she saw members from Bardizag, the location of the first school in Turkey under Elder AcMoody. They were her friends and students. She had lived with them and taught them. Now she could hardly recognize them. Most of the older members, the small children, and the weak had already perished along the road. Half of them, probably more, had died before they reached Eregli. How anyone could have the heart to force these skin-draped skeletons to continue the march was more than Diamondola could understand. Yet they were compelled step by step to march to the Syrian Desert. She knew that very few if any would ever make it, but that was the way the Turks meant it to be.

Diamondola walked from room to room in the inn searching for members, one drawn face with sunken eyes looked up into hers as she passed. Claw-like, bluish fingers reached out tremulously to touch her, and a weak voice sobbed, "Oh, Diamondola, is it you, or an angel from God? Come here, my child."

Diamondola turned and looked carefully into the sallow face framed by strands of matted hair. The dirty, blood-stained clothing reeked, and lice crawled freely over the gaunt frame. The woman's purple feet and legs, oozing with open sores, hardly looked human. Diamondola shook her head. "I do not know you, my sister. Who are you?" she asked evenly, trying to restrain her emotions. "I am Sister M– from Bardizag. Don't you remember you stayed with me the summer you were sick?"

Diamondola flung her arms around her and wept. What a change! Incredible! She had been one of the most active members in both the church and the community. She had a heart of gold, and had had a graceful, healthy body, fair skin, rosy full cheeks, sparkling gray eyes, and beautiful light-brown curly hair. She had been a strikingly beautiful woman. Had been! Was it possible that this repulsive creature, this half-dead, ghastly human wreck reclining on that evil-smelling pallet could be M——? M—— had been the best cook in Bardizag, and the epitome of cleanliness. Only in the weak voice could Diamondola detect a resemblance to her former friend.

"Oh, help me, Diamondola. Please save me. Take me with you back to Constantinople. I'm so tired. My husband is in the army, my two boys died along the way—one died clutching the last Memory Verse Card he had received in Bardizag. I couldn't bury him. But the angels marked his little body lying there in the ditch among the snow and weeds. The other boy froze to death. My twelve-year-old girl was beautiful, and was sold by the gendarme of my group to one of the Turkish villagers for a wife for one of his sons. Would to God that all of my children had died in infancy. My dead boys are better off than my girl in the harem. The boys, though only eight and ten, both had great faith. Please, Diamondola, either help me to go with you or help me to die here. I have been raped night after night by these godless gendarmes. I have smeared mud on my face to appear less attractive. I have not been able to bathe in weeks, and now I'm too starved to care. Pray that I will die quickly and suffer no longer."

Diamondola could find no words with which to express her feelings. But she did pray. A few days later the way to Allepo, Sister M——— fell by the roadside. Death seemed sweet to this child of God as she breathed her last. She did not feel the final kicks of her guard nor the bayonet that slashed open her abdomen in the hurried attempt to get off her belt and vest as he greedily sought for the gold coins he thought he might find there.

The end of M———'s family was typical of thousands of others. Each story Diamondola heard was as heart rending as the next. At times, she felt she could bear to see and hear no more. She found eating difficult, and her sleep at night was disturbed by gruesome nightmares of the atrocities her friends were suffering.

At Eregli the vice-governor heard that there was a German visitor in town. Wishing to honor his country's allies, he invited Elder Frauchiger and his translator to his home.

"Oh, you must not stay with the deportees in that horrible inn," he insisted. "You must stay with me in my home. You must eat at my table."

Elder Frauchiger explained that they appreciated his hospitality, but they were missionaries, and had come to visit their brethren who were being unjustly discriminated against because they were Armenians, regardless of their personal devotion to their country and their God. The vice-governor expressed sympathetic understanding and insisted that the missionaries come and spend some time in his home and tell him about the Adventist Christians. This the missionaries were happy to do. It gave them an opportunity to tell this influential man about God. They hoped that through him they might be able to secure the release of some of the Adventist deportees. When at last they met him, they presented the case of Christians in general, for they wished to see all exiles released.

The governor's home was palatial, and the exigencies of war had had little effect on his way of life. Being an important person, he had hoarded enough food and flour to supply his needs. The meal they ate at the vice-governor's table was the first real meal the missionaries had enjoyed since they had eaten with the Greek Orthodox patriarch. But the thought of the bark and dry grasses, soggy potatoes, and raw rice that the exiles were eating for supper that night took away the pleasure of the meal.

After supper, the vice-governor invited all the leading men in the city to come and hear the honored German guest speak. Diamondola, dressed in her navy blue, European-style suit, was the only woman in the room. The vice-governor never introduced her to his harem, nor did he invite even one veiled wife into the room to make the translator feel more at ease. The spacious room easily seated the fifty or more men who reclined on rich carpeted pads around three walls of the room. Diamondola and Elder Frauchiger and the vice-governor sat in chairs along the fourth wall. Elder Frauchiger spoke straight to the hearts of those Moslem leaders about God. He referred to our humane obligations and the judgment day. His listeners were impressed. Gladly would some of them have used their power to release those exiles from the filthy, broken-down inn. But since the orders for the death march had come from Constantinople, the minor officials of Eregli could do nothing about it.

When it was time to retire, the vice-governor showed Diamondola and Elder Frauchiger to a single room. This was embarrassing enough. But more embarrassing still, the vice-governor entered the room as well, and stood staring at Diamondola. Diamondola just sat down on her bed and waited for the governor to leave, but his deliberate lingering soon made it obvious that he had no intention of leaving. Elder Frauchiger led the way to the door and invited the vice-governor to follow him. But the vice-governor shook his head. He eyed Diamondola curiously. Finally he asked, "Why don't you hurry up and undress, young lady? I'm eager to see what you wear underneath those European tight clothes."

Diamondola was horrified but remained calm. She translated the questions to Elder Frauchiger and asked him what she should do. Elder Frauchiger was acquainted with the customs of that area and knew that as guests they must not offend their host.

"Diamondola," answered Frauchiger carefully, "take off your suit, crawl into bed as quickly as possible and cover up. Tonight you will have to sleep with all of your underclothes on. This is the last night we will spend here. Tomorrow night we will stay at the inn, even if we must live with the body lice and vermin. It is preferable to staying here. God will protect us there I'm sure."

Diamondola was embarrassed and humiliated. She turned her back and removed her outer clothes, then quickly slipped under the covers, which she had previously opened. This seemed to satisfy the vice-governor's curiosity, and he left the room. Elder Frauchiger then pulled his bed mat over against the door to make sure it remained closed the rest of the night, and lay down to sleep in his suit. He realized that it would not be safe to let Diamondola sleep alone in the room. They talked and prayed nearly all night. The next morning after breakfast they thanked their host for his hospitality and left.

The brethren at the inn were happy for their return, but they were bitterly disappointed when they learned that the workers had not secured their release. The exiles now realized that their case was hopeless, and they sank into utter despair. In a few days they were on the move again—to the desert and death. Very few survived.

Diamondola and Elder Frauchiger started back to Constantinople with heavy hearts. They felt that their missionary trip had been largely a failure. True, they had given the deportees relief, but they had not secured their release.

On their return Diamondola and Elder Frauchiger once again stopped at Iconium, Aksehir, and Eskishehir. They looked up new deportees and gave away their last gold coins, keeping scarcely enough to get them back home. The clothing and blankets had disappeared long before, but they did all they could to make the exiles comfortable. In Eskishehir they found the interested Greeks eager to hear more. Uncle Elisha and Uncle Stephanos seemed happy and relieved to see Diamondola return safely. They had not approved of this hazardous missionary, journey. Cousin Sava again opened his house, and the missionaries held a few more meetings. From Eskishehir they went to Smyrna and saw Dr. Girou and his wife. Because he was a dentist, Dr. Girou was able to do missionary work in this city. Here as elsewhere the only Adventists left in the cities were Greeks.

In the latter part of February, 1916, Elder Frauchiger and Diamondola arrived back in Constantinople. The church members gathered around them with anxious questions. "Did you find our members? Were you able to help them? Did you save them from deportation?" they asked.

Elder Frauchiger turned his head to hide his tears. What could they answer? Diamondola tried to sum up the results of the trip slowly and deliberately as she struggled to control her emotions.

"We found many of the members," she said. "The Armenian members were nearly all with the exiles. They were grateful for your clothing and money, which helped alleviate some of their suffering. But we could not save them from the death march. Nevertheless, praise God, they were faithful."

The atrocities committed against Christian people by the Ottoman Turks are often spoken of most critically by Western nations. However, modern civilized man's "inhumanity to man" in Europe and Asia during World War II makes one less critical of past generations and realize that it is only God's ruling and restraining power that prevents men from annihilating humanity from this earth.

## CHAPTER XXVI
# Tasting His Goodness

*"O taste and see that the Lord is good:*
*blessed is the man that trusteth in him" (Ps. 34:8).*

It was still winter in Constantinople, and Diamondola was back again at the office. Her mind was kept busy during the day with the office work, but at night she would awaken from horrible nightmares, in which she would be seeing the deportees starving and pleading for her help. Sometimes she would dream she was sleeping again with the refugees, or trekking with them on the horror-filled road to extermination. Some nights as she lay awake in her bed she would think of Ares. Correspondence was so infrequent that it made the months of waiting for his return seem longer. It had been nearly two years since their engagement, and it seemed ages since she had heard from him. She wondered whether he had heard of her imprisonment the summer before. She was sure he had not heard of her trip to the interior with Elder Frauchiger. A letter from Alexandra had come through via Germany. She had hinted that Ares was not well, and Diamondola was worried about him. However, because he had been so healthy, she felt sure he would soon recover.

Diamondola had lived such a crowded life and had passed through so many experiences that she had learned that truly "all things work together for good to them that love God." She could see His guiding hand in her life and she knew He was overruling in all the affairs of His people. The war might be prolonged, Ares might be sick, and God's people might be suffering persecution and death, but God was still ruler over all things.

Food was becoming increasingly scarce in Turkey. All the good wheat grown in Turkey was exported to Germany. The same was true of many of the other nourishing foods, such as dried legumes, potatoes, and rice. Theodora searched out the poor and the sick among the church members and gave them of her rice and milk supplies. Many people were benefited by her farsightedness in laying in supplies of rice and milk. Some who had scarcely enough to keep soul and body together were fed weekly at Theodora's table. Two old church members who were especially destitute were fed regularly every week. Like the widow of Elijah's day, Theodora's milk and rice supply never seemed to run out.

One morning Diamondola opened the office door and discovered that the place had been ransacked. Soon Brother Bridde arrived and the two investigated the damage. It was evident that someone had come in and examined many of the mission papers and files but apparently had taken nothing. Diamondola went into her office to begin her work for the day, but she quickly realized that one of her three typewriters was missing. It was the English typewriter. "Brother Bridde," she called, "they've taken my English typewriter. Now what shall we do? It can never be replaced until the war is over. And then, will we have the money?"

Paul Bridde was deeply concerned. How difficult it would be for them to do by hand the work usually done by their English typewriter!

"Let us kneel down right here and ask God to send the typewriter back to us. He knows where it is, and He can impress the thief to bring it back."

"But, Brother Bridde," questioned Diamondola, "is it fair to pray this way?"

"Of course it is," he answered with conviction. "All the mission property belongs to God, and we can expect Him to look after it. He knows our needs. Let us pray. God will send it back."

The two workers knelt then and there and prayed. Then they rose and went about their regular work. All day long Diamondola expected the typewriter to reappear, but it did not. When she went to the office the next morning she thought surely it would have been returned during the night.

But the typewriter was not in its usual place. The third day both workers began to wonder whether their prayer would be answered as they had expected, or whether God had some other plan in mind. But they were willing to wait on the Lord and accept His answer.

Paul Bridde went to the post office to get the mail. Diamondola was left alone in the office. Suddenly there was a short, sharp knock on the door. Diamondola put down the last few words of the sentence she was translating and went to answer the door. As she opened the door, something leaning against it fell at her feet with a familiar clatter. She glanced up just in time to see a poorly clad porter disappear around the corner. Diamondola was dumfounded. Bending over, she pulled a gunny sack with its contents into the hallway and closed the door against the chill March winds. It was the English typewriter. She was overjoyed. Mustering all her strength, she lifted the heavy old machine out of the bag and set it on the desk. Then she put a piece of paper in the roller and tried it. It worked as well as ever. When Paul Bridde returned from the post office he found Diamondola hard at work typing some letters. His face lighted up at the sight.

"You see, God did send it back. Now I hope that the letter H doesn't stick anymore."

"It doesn't," Diamondola answered. "Let us thank God for this miracle." And they did.

April, 1916, came, and the time was set for another baptism. Tcharakian was overjoyed, for among the baptismal candidates was his old friend Aram Ashod. Ashod had passed through many trials. He was the sole support of his sister and father, and getting a job during the troublesome days of the war was not easy. The problem was compounded by his resolve to keep the Sabbath holy. He lost one good job as bookkeeper in a department store, but he held fast to the promise that God would never leave him nor forsake him.

The Sabbath the baptism was held was dismal. The Adventist group met secretly on the Marmara Sea. In spite of the inclement weather, the ravages of the war, and terrible persecution, the brotherhood of Christians felt the peace and joy that passes all understanding.

Tcharakian saw in Ashod the possibilities of a future worker, and Elder Frauchiger agreed that a man such as Ashod, with his business experience and training, could fit nicely into the Adventist work. However, in order to render the most effective service the first step would be for him to learn

English, and become more familiar with the Adventist doctrines. Tcharakian insisted that Diamondola teach him English. So it was that Aram became Diamondola's new missionary project. Aram's father was angry because of his son's new faith, and declared he had become an Adventist because of the pretty little office secretary.

In order to prove that this was not so, Aram one day invited the whole office staff, including the Frauchigers, Diamondola and Mother Keanides, Tcharakian, and Paul Bridde for dinner. In the presence of his father, Aram inquired in a voice loud enough for all to hear, "And how is your fiancé, Ares? I hope you hear from him soon and that he will return before long for your marriage."

Aram's father looked with disbelief at Diamondola. "Are you engaged?" he asked.

"Yes," she answered simply. "I have been engaged for more than two years. As soon as the war is over my fiancé will return and we will be married."

"Well," said the puzzled old father shaking his head, "I thought if Aram were interested in you, he at least had some sensible excuse for becoming a Sabbatarian."

During the months from May to December, while he was out of work, Aram translated *The Great Controversy* into Turkish for the benefit of his sister and father. Aram learned English quickly. Diamondola was proud of his excellent progress, and looked forward with joy to the lessons every evening.

Elder Baharian had been sent that summer to the interior. The office had been anxiously awaiting word from him about the church members. The names of the members whom Diamondola knew of a certainty were dead, she removed from the church books.

She worried much that summer because she was not hearing from Ares and she knew he had been sick. Besides this trial, every day seemed to bring the depressing news that some other dear member or friend had died on the death march.

Added to all these burdens came the shocking news one day of Elder Baharian's death. Perhaps it was shortsighted on the part of the mission to have sent him to the interior. Though he was a minister of the gospel, he was an Armenian too, and thus subject to the same persecution being meted out to his fellow countrymen. Eventually the inevitable happened. It was reported that one day he ran into the wrong government official.

Suspected of being an insurrectionist because of his contacts with the deportees, he was being taken by gendarmes from one village to another when he was shot. Baharian laid down his life out on a lonely Turkish road with a bullet through his back. He had worked tirelessly until his last moments for the salvation of his people as well as of the Turks.

Diamondola and her mother mourned with the rest of the church over his death. He was the spiritual father of all the early members in Turkey, and his death brought great sorrow and discouragement to the church. Yet God had raised up in his stead a man as strong and as faithful and zealous as Baharian. That man was Diran Tcharakian. Though abandoned by his family and his friends, he picked up the banner of truth and went fearlessly forward, bringing the message of salvation into the homes of the rich and influential, the Moslem and the Christian. He fired the members with renewed enthusiasm.

"Why should we falter now as we near the end of the race?" he said. "Baharian did his work and God gave him rest from his labors. What have you done to deserve rest? Will you stand idle in sorrow because you wanted Baharian to do all the soul saving? Jesus told the disciples to go back to Jerusalem and work after He left them. Your commission is the same. We must go back to Constantinople, and throughout all Turkey, and work. Baharian is dead, but God's message is not. Go out to the harvest, my brethren and sisters. The sickle has been thrust into our hands through the death of our brother." And so the church went back to work with renewed vigor, and God blessed it.

Late that summer food became scarcer than ever. One morning Theodora confessed, "I'm afraid that I have given away too much rice and milk, for we are nearly out of food ourselves. This is Wednesday night and the two old members will come for their usual weekly meal. What shall I give them? Prices have gone so high that I am already out of the food money for the month. Winter is coming, and what shall we do?"

Diamondola was shocked by the serious tone in her mother's voice. Since Mother had come to live with her, she had never worried about where her food came from. Mother had managed admirably.

"Let's pray about it, Mother," she finally said. "I'm completely out of cash, but God will provide. If not, we'll just go hungry a few days until payday."

God did provide, however, and in an unexpected way. Uncle Stephanos' eldest son, Gabriel, who was twenty years old, worked for the Toros

Express railroad. One day Gabriel called from the station and asked Diamondola if she could come over and pick up some things his father had sent for Theodora.

Soon Diamondola and cousin Gabriel were back at the house. Uncle Stephanos had sent a few sacks of wheat and rice from his land. Though Theodora was grateful for the food, she was even happier for the meaning the gift represented. It meant that Diamondola's visit to Uncle Stephanos seven months before had accomplished some good. It meant that he was once more Theodora's brother. It meant that he loved his sister, and was concerned for her. When Gabriel left the house Diamondola and her mother knelt and thanked God for the food He had sent to them and for the change in the heart of the giver. A wave of emotion swept over Theodora. She wept as she pleaded with God for the conversion of her only living brother, who had suddenly shown his love to her. It was evident that she wished to be alone, so Diamondola discreetly slipped out of the room and down to her office. As she worked she thought of her experiences through the past twenty-two and a half years of her life. Truly, whenever she had prayed, God had always answered, and had led her in ways that she herself would have chosen if she could have seen the end from the beginning.

As she was meditating on God's wonderful providences, Aram Ashod burst into the office in great excitement.

"Oh, Diamondola," he exclaimed, "I've got wonderful news. You know I have been without work since May. Well, I have just finished reading *Great Controversy* through to my father and sister and she has accepted the truth. And now I have found a job. It pays much more than the former job. I am so thrilled. God's blessings are not just showers, but real cloudbursts. My sister's conversion should have been enough, but now this job—well, it's just fantastic. It's God's mercy." Tears of thankfulness and joy coursed down Aram's cheeks.

"Brother Aram," she said, "we also have just received a blessing from God's bountiful hand. My Uncle Stephanos has been estranged from us for many years. Now he sent his son with food for us, just when we needed it most. But the blessing of the food is not as important to us as his change of spirit. I am not more thrilled for you over your new job than I am to hear of your success in winning your sister to the remnant church. 'O taste and see that the Lord is good'!"

"Yes, and His mercy endureth forever," added Ashod. Nineteen sixteen had been a year of tragedies, deaths, hunger, and perplexities, but it had also been a year of blessings. Aram Ashod had been added to the church along with many others, the stolen typewriter had been returned, and food had arrived just in time to help feed some of the hungry members. Now Aram had a good job, and he had the joy of having his sister join him in the church.

There was no peace on earth that Christmas, but there was peace in the hearts of these believers. The world lacked the feeling of good will toward men, but the faithful members in Constantinople looked forward to the day when good will would fill the earth made new. The past year had strengthened their faith and their courage, and they looked forward to the time when they would no longer count time by years. It was good that Diamondola could not see the tragedy that the coming year would bring—a tragedy so severe that only the utmost faith in God would see her through.

## CHAPTER XXVII
# *Knowing and Accepting*

*"Be still, and know that I am God" (Ps. 46:10).*
*"Precious in the sight of the Lord is the death of his saints" (Ps. 116:15).*

Diamondola found that work was a real blessing to her during the bleak winter of 1917.

Her busy routine gave her little time to think of the problems that disturbed her mind during her few hours of relaxation. One burden that weighed especially heavy upon her heart was her inability to communicate with her fiancé. She hadn't heard from Ares in more than a year. The one truly happy part of the day, however, had been the evening when she gave Ashod his English lesson. But now there were rumors that a new draft call was about to be made. Those who had previously purchased their freedom were required to re-enlist. This would take both Tcharakian and Ashod and many others like them. But there was work, always work, to banish these morbid thoughts from Diamondola's mind. Her naturally buoyant spirit refused to be dampened by the continuous perplexities of life. Somehow the sun always dispelled the shadows of sorrow and uncertainty.

One day Elder Frauchiger received a letter from Germany that intrigued her. During the early part of the war the letters from the division office in Hamburg often contained news of the workers throughout the field. As Diamondola handed Elder Frauchiger the letter from Hamburg, she felt like asking him to open it quickly and tell her what it said about Ares and Alexandra. But she had the good sense to excuse herself from Elder Frauchiger's office and wait for him to reveal any contents of the letter that might pertain to her loved ones. Back in her office she found herself trembling with excitement—waiting to hear news about two of the dearest people on earth to her. She was still sitting on the edge of her chair when Elder Frauchiger's door opened.

She leaped to her feet with eager anticipation, but Frauchiger brushed past her, his face clouded and pale, his lips pursed and silent. It was hard for Diamondola to work the rest of the morning. She wondered what the letter contained that had so disturbed Elder Frauchiger. He had become like a father to her and they had shared many joys and sorrows in the work of God together, but now he was silent. She knew him well enough to understand that only news of a tragedy could draw him out of the office and away from his work. Although spring had arrived, the day was dismal, and dark forebodings clouded the office that morning. Diamondola spent most of the morning staring out into space and wondering, "Oh, why doesn't Elder Frauchiger share his trials with me! I would be glad to try to cheer him up as he has always tried to help me."

That afternoon the sun broke through the overcast sky and Elder Frauchiger returned to the office. He asked Diamondola to go for a walk with him and his daughter. Diamondola was only too happy to do this. Their families had often shared pleasant outings together. Diamondola tried to make conversation as the three walked along the nearly deserted streets, but Elder Frauchiger seemed reluctant to speak. When they reached a quiet place near the outskirts of Constantinople, Elder Frauchiger turned to Diamondola and placed his hand on her shoulder.

"Diamondola," he began solemnly. His tone frightened her. "I have some bad news for you. But first, tell me, my child, do you believe that God knows what is best for you?"

"Yes," she gulped as fear clutched her breast.

"And do you believe that God will send a blessing with every disappointment?" he continued.

"I think I do. But what is the news? Please, I cannot stand the suspense any longer. Is it about my sister, or—Ares?"

"Diamondola, I received word today from Germany that Ares is dead."

"Dead?" she repeated, too stunned to realize what had happened. "Dead?" she repeated, then asked, "Not sick?"

"He died about six months ago, Diamondola, but with the war situation news travels so very slowly—even from Greece to Turkey. Your sister Alexandra sent the message through our office in Germany. I didn't know how to break the news to you. We all feel sorry to lose Ares, but I know you feel our loss the keenest. May God help you."

Diamondola clutched her throat. It seemed that she could not breathe. She felt faint. The world seemed to spin and the sun faded out. Elder Frauchiger and his daughter took Diamondola by the arms and led her to the Frauchiger home. She felt cold and faint, and her pulse was weak. Her heart seemed to have turned to stone. She could not swallow the warm drink offered her. Her body and mind seemed paralyzed. She seemed unable to accept the fact that God, who had loved her so much, had permitted the man she loved to be taken away by death. Why, oh, why? She wanted to ask the question, but her lips would not form the words. She lay down on the davenport, closed her eyes, and tried to think and pray. The Frauchiger family, though their hearts were breaking with hers and for her, very wisely closed the door as she requested and left her alone.

Several hours later Diamondola rose from the davenport. "I'm going home to mother," she announced quietly. "Please do not tell her of this tragedy. I do not want her to worry and weep about it. It is enough that I know. Later, when I gain the courage, I will tell her."

"Diamondola," pleaded Elder Frauchiger, "do not try to bear your tragedy alone. Let others share your sorrow with you, and it will seem lighter. Now we know that God has another plan in store for you. We must wait and see what it is."

*But I do not want another plan,* Diamondola thought rebelliously. *Ares and I waited patiently for almost three years to have our plans fulfilled. It was our feeling of obligation to the work of God that kept us from fulfilling our plans sooner. Maybe I should have married him and gone to Greece. Maybe he wouldn't have gotten sick and died of tuberculosis if I had been with him.*

Thus she thought, but to the Frauchigers she said, her lips trembling, "Yes, I'll have to see—good night."

Diamondola fled through the deserted streets, crying abandonedly. She had easily accepted her father's death, for he had suffered many years. But Ares was so young, so vigorous, so full of love and confidence in God.

"Why, God, why?" she screamed aloud as she looked up into the moonlit sky.

The words flashed back to her like a correction from the Almighty, "BE STILL, AND KNOW THAT I AM GOD." Be still.

Who was she, feeble little earthling as she was, to shout accusations at God? Was Ares more precious to her than he was to God? And though she wished that she could have died in his stead, why should she question God's justice? Perhaps it was because there was yet a work for her to do, and Ares' work was done. Perhaps he was at rest now because he was more ready than she. He would never have reacted in this manner. Now she was thoroughly ashamed of her behavior, and she begged for the forgiveness and mercy of God once more.

"O my God," she sobbed humbly as she knelt on the cold cobblestones, "I believe; help Thou my unbelief. Forgive, I pray, my resentment and my grief. Help me to bear my sorrow as a child of Thine should. Help me, oh, help me. Amen."

She walked slowly home. Tears of true grief and humble repentance coursed down her pale cheeks. By the time she reached home, she had made her peace with God. She climbed the five flights of steps laboriously, for the shock she had sustained left her weak. As she opened the door, Mother called to her from her bed. "Diamondola, my child, I'm glad you're back home. Is anything wrong?" she inquired anxiously.

"No, Mother," Diamondola replied; "everything is all right now."

And it was. Diamondola had accepted her sorrow, and with God leading the way, she knew everything would be all right. She could not see the end from the beginning, but she was certain that God, who could, had made provision for her future.

Sabbath morning arrived. "Diamondola, should I have someone else translate for me today?" asked Elder Frauchiger solicitously. "I must announce to our church members the death of our brother Ares, and I realize that this would be too difficult for you."

"No, I will translate today as usual," answered Diamondola firmly. "This will be my last service to Ares. He would not want me to mourn as do others who have no hope of the resurrection. He lived only for service to God, and translating is my service. I will not shirk my duty. Besides, who else here could translate today? You know there is no one else, and so do I. Let us go on with the service as planned, and God will help me bear up under my sorrow. I have accepted God's way already, as you know. Shall I lead the way onto the platform?"

"Yes," he said trying to hide his own tears. He could see by the determined look in her face that she had the courage for the crisis. "And God bless you," he added.

During the announcements Diamondola translated unwaveringly the details of Ares' death. There was not a dry eye in the congregation, and some were weeping audibly. Tcharakian and Ashod shook their heads sorrowfully and wept for the brave-hearted girl who had been called upon to suffer such a terrible tragedy and yet faced her loss with such courage.

## CHAPTER XXVIII
## *"Tabitha, Arise"*

*"But Peter put them all forth, and kneeled down, and prayed; and turning him to the body said, Tabitha, arise. And she opened her eyes: ... and sat up. And he gave her his hand, and lifted her up, and when he had called the saints and widows, presented her alive. ... And many believed in the Lord"* (Acts 9:40–42).

Brother Tcharakian and Ashod were back in the army. Both of them, as well as other Adventists, were having Sabbath problems. After Diamondola's last experience in writing letters to Tcharakian while he was in his country's service, she hardly knew whether she dared write to the Adventist soldiers. But since she had to write the mission letters, which Elder Frauchiger signed, her letters did continue to cheer the isolated members and soldiers.

By 1917 most soldiers in Turkey and Germany began to feel that they were fighting a losing battle, and it was hard to keep up their morale. The war-weary citizens could also sense the signs of the end of the conflict. At the same time the world was watching America, and when she entered the conflict on the side of the Allies, the outcome was a foregone conclusion.

*Left to right: Brother Tefronides, colporteur; Professor Tcharakian; Brother Bridde, treasurer; Elder Frauchiger; and Diamondola.*

With this new political development, the division asked Elder Frauchiger in 1917 to move to Yugoslavia. It was felt that a German-speaking man carrying a neutral Swiss passport could do more to advance the work of the church than a man who did not have these qualifications. So, Paul Bridde and Diamondola were left to carry on the work alone until a new man could arrive. This change was one more heartbreak for Diamondola. The Frauchigers had become a part of her family. She especially missed Elder Frauchiger, upon whom she had learned to depend as a father after the death of her own father. But the work of God must go forward, and she and Bridde accepted the burden. Now there were just two workers left in the whole of Turkey—Bridde and Diamondola.

The two men who could have helped in the ministry were in the army. Aram Ashod was stationed near Constantinople. From his immediate superior he had succeeded in getting his Sabbaths off and thus was able to assist with the Sabbath services. But his real test came when he was forced to bear arms. Once he was beaten, until he was rescued by an officer who took pity on him. On another occasion, he was forced to stand guard for an hour with a dagger in his belt and a soldier pointing a bayonet at his side. When he wrote to his superiors asking to be relieved from bearing arms, and his request finally reached the pasha, the answer came back, "Make the soldier obey and carry arms." The church members concluded that Aram Ashod would be the next member who would be missing from their congregation.

They were right. The next Sabbath, Ashod was not in the meeting hall. Later Diamondola learned that Ashod was missing from church, not because of his refusal to bear arms, but because his unit had been moved to fight on the Syrian border. His unit was there only a few months when they were captured by the British Army. He was marched with his fellow prisoners to Gaza, and later to Cairo. How many survived the trek was never known. Back in Constantinople, Ashod was reported missing in action, as were also the rest of the men in his unit. Diamondola left his name on the books, hoping that he might be among the survivors. In the fall of 1917 Henry Erzberger arrived in Constantinople from the Syrian Mission. Since he had learned Arabic, and was now in a different language area, Diamondola had to continue her translation work for the new missionary. The Erzbergers shared the same flat with the Keanides, and they soon became fast friends.

November, 1918, saw the terrible war brought to an end. For Turkey and Germany it meant defeat and depression. Both countries lost lands and possessions and millions of their young men. But everyone was glad that the war was over, and they hoped that life would resume a normal pattern.

With the Armistice came more changes within the mission office in Turkey. Paul Bridde, though an Adventist, was a German, and hence was invited to return to his fatherland by the nations working out the peace settlements. He was given one week to leave Turkey. That week was spent in teaching Diamondola the intricacies of bookkeeping. After just one week of these specialized lessons she became the secretary-treasurer of the Levant Union Mission.

Toward the end of the year the mission learned that Ashod was still living. He was attending church in Cairo with the Keoughs and Bezirdjians. "Someday," be wrote, "I hope to return to Turkey and join the work of God."

Tcharakian had also survived the war and was back at work. Besides him there were only two other ministers who had survived the deportations and war. Almost a dozen other faithful ministers had laid down their lives during the war years. Diamondola tallied the membership of the church in Turkey at the beginning of the new year and found that in spite of the new additions it was less than half the number in 1914.

In April, 1919, the church members who had survived the massacres and deportation began arriving in Constantinople. Christians of all faiths were forsaking their houses and lands in the interior and heading for Constantinople. Here they hoped that the Red Cross and other philanthropic organizations would help them to emigrate to American or European countries. Most organizations had large churches, which they turned into refugee centers, but the Adventists had only the few office rooms, and the dark twelve by twenty-foot church room on the first floor, plus the apartments of the Erzberger and Keanides families on the fifth floor. In between lived three floors of non-Adventist renters. The building was only leased to the Adventists, and they had no money with which to rent more space.

The few Adventist survivors were in need of medical and nursing care and nourishment. The refugees were mostly children in their early teens and some young women. Because of the deprivation or cruel treatment, they had experienced, most of them were physical wrecks. The refugees were made as comfortable as possible in the first-floor offices and in the meeting hall. Theodora, Diamondola, and Mrs. Erzberger spent many hours running up and down the flights of steps from their apartments with warm water for treatments, special diets, and medications. Elder Erzberger, too, became dangerously ill with dysentery. With this development, the three women were left to carry on alone the mission work, the home work, and the refugee work.

One younger sister in the church who had small children became very ill. She was placed on a mat in the office, and became Diamondola's special charge. Because of the seriousness of her condition Diamondola sat by her side and cared for her, while the children were cared for by the women upstairs.

"Please take care of my children," she sobbed one day. "I am dying. Just give me one more drink of water."

Diamondola raised the woman's head so that she could sip the water more easily from the cup in her hand. But she never took the drink. She died in Diamondola's hands, a victim of typhus.

Three days later Diamondola began to run a fever. It soon was apparent that she had typhus too. As she lay tossing feverishly in the bed, Mother washed her body and found a large body louse, the carrier of the disease.

For six weeks Diamondola's temperature ranged between 103 and 105. Subsisting entirely on liquids, she became a wasted skeleton. Even her dearest friends hardly recognized her as daily she grew worse. At last she drifted into a coma. For three days, she scarcely showed any signs of life. Mrs. Erzberger, who was a nurse, spent many hours by Diamondola's side. One day as she stood by Diamondola's bed she noticed a complete lack of activity. She had nursed many patients in her lifetime and had watched them as they drifted off into the valley of death. It always made her feel sad. But it was harder for her this time since it was a dear friend. She searched desperately for the slightest indication of pulse beat, yet she knew all the while that there was none.

Mrs. Erzberger, choking with emotion, called Theodora. "Come quickly, I'm afraid that Diamondola has drifted into her final sleep. There is no pulse. I have felt everywhere—neck, head, hand."

Theodora was stunned. She had felt so certain that Diamondola would live. She had never doubted that her daughter would one day get well. True, the doctor had kept telling her that Diamondola's case was hopeless, but Theodora had never believed him.

At last she stammered, "Well, if you say so, Mrs. Erzberger, you must be right. But wait," she paused, grasping at a thin straw of hope, "there is still another way of finding this out. Get a candle and hold it by her nose. If it flickers, she is still breathing. Please hurry."

But even as she spoke she turned and looked at the still, wasted form lying in the bed, and all hope faded. Theodora took Diamondola's bony hand in her own and kissed the still, cold fingers. Tears stung her eyes, but she blinked them back resolutely.

Mrs. Erzberger arrived with the candle and matches. She lighted the candle and held it close to Diamondola's nose. There was not the least flicker. Diamondola was dead. The two women stood silently by the bed and wept.

Presently a call from Mr. Erzberger brought them back to reality. This was no time to give way to grief. There was much that had to be done. The house was full of refugees, some of them young orphans, and Mr. Erzberger was still a very sick patient.

"Please send us help, O God," prayed Mrs. Erzberger. "I cannot tell my husband just now of Diamondola's death; he is still too sick. We need help to arrange for the funeral. Send us help, someone—a man to help us at this time."

Mrs. Erzberger continued praying silently as she hurried about caring for the needs of the other patients. Mrs. Keanides suppressed her sobs, not wanting to upset the others. After the needs of the living were cared for, she laid out the burial clothes for Diamondola over the foot of the bed. It was the law in Turkey that bodies must be buried within twenty-four hours after death. Theodora and Mrs. Erzberger felt overwhelmed at the multitudinous tasks that had to be done before the time limit expired. How could they alone make all the necessary arrangements before the funeral?

Theodora also prayed, "O Lord, send someone to help us—someone to buy the coffin and prepare the grave. We need human help. But please bring comfort to my soul and help me to understand."

A short while later there was a knock at the door. Mrs. Erzberger opened the door and burst into tears when she saw it was Tcharakian. He seemed to her like an angel sent from heaven. No one else could have filled their needs better in that hour than Tcharakian—the man of faith and courage and comfort, the friend of God and the friend to man.

"Why the tears, sister?" he asked in a comforting tone of voice.

"Diamondola—she is dead!" sobbed Mrs. Erzberger.

"Dead? Diamondola is dead?" he asked, momentarily stunned. When he had recovered he said, "No, I cannot believe she is really dead. This is incredible. God needs her for His work just now. This is not the time for her to die. She is the secretary-treasurer, she is the only fluent translator the mission has, and she has been the binding influence in the work during this period of rehabilitation. No," he paused again, "I cannot believe that it is God's will for her to die now."

"But," objected Mrs. Erzberger in dismay, "how can you talk like that? She is dead. Dead, I tell you. She is not the first dead person I've seen, and I have used every test to be sure she is not alive."

"Oh, this may be true," agreed Tcharakian nodding his head. "She may be dead, but she doesn't need to stay dead. Peter prayed to God, and in the name of the Lord, Dorcas arose from the dead. My dear sister, God knows our every need. If God still needs Diamondola in His work, and if her mother still needs her help, God is glorified through our faith in His power to resurrect. Let us go into her room and pray."

Mrs. Erzberger was speechless. She dried her tears and followed him into Diamondola's room. His presence seemed to electrify the atmosphere with holy, elevating faith. His confidence in God was contagious, and Mrs. Erzberger seemed to sense that something was going to happen in the presence of such faith.

At the sight of Tcharakian, Theodora dried her tears and extended a hand of wordless welcome. Tcharakian grasped her hand in both of his, saying, "I know this death has been a difficult experience for you, Sister Keanides, but Diamondola is not dead. She is sleeping. We will pray now and see if God desires to resurrect her. Now, before we kneel, do either of you doubt that God is able, if He is willing, to resurrect Sister Diamondola?"

Both women shook their heads. It seemed almost irreverent to speak. They knelt with Elder Tcharakian as he prayed. The room seemed to fill with the presence of God and holy beings. Tcharakian closed his prayer, thanking God for answering him, then stood and walked to the bed. Taking hold of Diamondola's lifeless hand, he addressed her directly, "My dear Sister Diamondola, do you believe that Jesus can resurrect you? In the name of Jesus Christ, I say unto you, arise."

Both women, still kneeling, opened their eyes and looked toward the bed. They saw Diamondola's body quiver, a surge of blood seemed to course through her veins, her eyelids flickered, and she sat up in bed.

"Yes, Lord, yes." She spoke distinctly, looking up toward heaven. Then she rubbed her eyes and looked at Tcharakian standing by her side.

She smiled at him as he murmured, "Thank You, Jesus."

Diamondola then looked compassionately at her faithful nurses. "Do not doubt, do not doubt. I am resurrected!" she exclaimed, without ever having been told that it was so. "But, please," she begged, "I am so hungry. Could one of you bring me some milk?"

"Bring her some milk," Elder Tcharakian commanded in a kindly voice to the women still kneeling on the floor. They arose together and in unison walked out the door. What had happened seemed unbelievable.

In a few minutes the women returned with the warm milk, still awed and silent Diamondola sensed the grief and shock that these dear ones had recently passed through, so she urged, "Let us sing 'At the Door.'"

The three joined her as they sang over and over, "At the door, at the door, At the door, yes, even at the door; He is coming, He is coming, He is even at the door."

## CHAPTER XXIX
# *Honey Hastens Recovery*

> *"My son, eat thou honey, because it is good;
> and the honeycomb, which is sweet to thy taste" (Prov. 24:13).*

Diamondola was thrilled at the miracle that had happened to her. But there was a period of recovery ahead that no one had anticipated. Why didn't God restore her to complete health and strength at once? That is a question that Diamondola would like to have asked God, but, whatever the reason, she was thankful for what the Lord had done for her.

During the months of recovery in the summer and autumn of 1919 Diamondola's principal comfort and joy was to hear the Bible read to her. She also memorized many passages of Scripture that proved invaluable later on in her ministry.

Mrs. Erzberger and Theodora Keanides were driven to the point of exhaustion from the extra work that was thrust upon them, so a special nurse, Miss Vosilika, was hired to care for Diamondola and the patients who were most seriously ill. After having laboratory tests made she decided to put Diamondola on a diet of milk.

However, Elder Tcharakian did not agree that this regimen was the best for the patient. It was his custom to call on Diamondola several times a day. On one of these visits Tcharakian brought a jar of honey in one pocket and plain, slightly sweet cookies in the other. Contrary to the nurse's orders Tcharakian fed Diamondola cookies dipped in honey, and soon she felt her strength returning. After three days the nurse ordered another laboratory test, and was greatly pleased to discover that the report indicated significant improvement in the patient. Tcharakian and Diamondola then told her their secret. The nurse chuckled and said, "Let's continue the milk diet—and the honey and cookies."

After lying on her back more than two months, Diamondola became conscious of a severe pain in her lower back, where an oozing sore had developed. Dr. Dinanian, who was treating her, called at the home one day and examined the source of complaint.

"You have a bad sore on your back. It will take a long time to heal," he said.

Outside the room the doctor revealed to the nurse and Tcharakian the seriousness of Diamondola's condition. He said that Diamondola had a large bedsore on her coccyx, which had become gangrenous. Her recovery, he said, would be difficult, for blackish flesh already was sloughing off from the sore. He recommended cleansing it each day with peroxide, and then pouring on a bit of iodine mixed with water.

Diamondola was treated exactly as the doctor had prescribed. The peroxide ran from the large hole on one side through some unknown passage, and out through an open sore on the other side of the backbone. Her backbone itself was exposed, and the only way Diamondola could endure the pain was to sleep on a soft ring that supported her body in such a way that the sores did not touch the bed. The most painful part of the whole experience was the iodine. For three days Diamondola patiently endured the treatment while the nurse removed the pieces of dead flesh that dropped onto the rubber sheet under her. The third day it was too much.

"O God," she cried in pain, "I can endure this treatment no longer. Please love me a little more and remove the pain."

Brother Tcharakian, standing outside the door, heard this plaintive cry of the sufferer. His tender heart was torn with pity. After the treatment, he walked back into the room.

"Nurse," he said, "I want you to follow the Biblical medication for this gang-" he checked himself as he almost spilled the secret, then said, "bedsore. We will use no more peroxide and iodine. We will pour a little wine and oil into the sores each day."

Everyone instinctively had confidence in Tcharakian, for he spoke as one who had authority straight from the mouth of God.

"All right," Miss Vosilika agreed readily. "Will you show me how to give the treatment tomorrow? After that I can do it alone." The next day Tcharakian treated Diamondola's sores with sterilized wine and oil. It was like the balm of Gilead, and soothed her painful sores.

The next few weeks the patient made steady improvement as the nurse continued the wine and oil treatment. At last the wine and oil no longer ran through the passage from one sore to the other. The diameter of the black patch shrank from six inches down to five, then four. New skin and flesh grew over the backbone again, and soon the two holes were completely separated and began healing separately.

As she convalesced Diamondola spent many hours talking to her nurse. At night when the pain was so severe that she was unable to sleep, they studied the Bible together. Her nurse was a Protestant engaged to an Orthodox young man. Elder Tcharakian convinced Miss Vosilika that it was unwise to yoke herself with one not of her faith. Before the summer ended she had broken her engagement and had become a full-fledged Seventh-day Adventist. Also by the end of the summer a letter came from Despina.

During the war years, she had had opportunity to go to America to complete her education. During the summer of 1919 she had graduated from her nurse's training course at Washington Sanitarium and Hospital. Diamondola was thrilled with this news—at last her younger sister had achieved her goal. How well she deserved it! The sacrificing Despina had worked so faithfully and uncomplainingly while Diamondola had completed her high school education.

But the second page of Despina's letter contained more exciting news. Despina was going to California. Mr. and Mrs. Govreckian, from Bardizag, were living in California. They heard that Despina had graduated from the nurse's course, and remembered her as the sweet and lovely younger sister of Diamondola. They invited her to come to live with them, and get acquainted with their son, Nazereth, who was a medical student at Loma Linda. The implication seemed obvious.

The Govreckians, who had changed their tongue-twisting name to Crisp for the benefit of the Americans, still clung to their Eastern customs.

They wanted to choose the bride for their son, but since the young people had become Americanized, this might not be so easy. So the Crisps tactfully invited Despina to come and be with them, "for old times' sake." Nursing was as pleasant in California as anywhere else—and besides, if Despina wanted to take some other specialized course, Loma Linda was the place and the Crisps would foot the bill, the letter read.

Despina saw through the plot, and in true Eastern fashion wrote and asked her mother, and especially Diamondola, who knew the Govreckians well, what they thought of the plan.

Diamondola was all for it, and so was Mother. So they wrote back immediately recommending that Despina marry Nazereth—provided, of course, that the two fell in love with each other.

A few months later a letter arrived from California bearing the following name on the return address: Mrs. Nazereth Crisp. Diamondola's joy knew no bounds, and every guest who entered her room for days was told the exciting news whether they knew Despina or not.

"Do you know," she would ask in that I've-got-a-secret tone, "Despina is married to Nazereth?"

In the autumn Diamondola was well enough so that she no longer needed a nurse. A few days later she and Mrs. Erzberger made a trip to Dr. Dinanian's office. "Do you remember this girl?" asked Mrs. Erzberger.

"No, I can't say that I do, but I think I recognize you as the Adventist missionary—"

"Yes, I am. And this is Diamondola Keanides—the girl who had a large gangrenous sore on her back. Do you remember you thought her case was hopeless?"

Dr. Dinanian scrutinized the rosy-cheeked, smiling figure before him. What a change from the pinched, pale skeleton with the shaved head that he had seen three months before.

"Well, I declare!" he exclaimed. "I never would have had any hope for her recovery, but God seems to perform special miracles for you Adventists. I wish I had the power of your Tcharakian. If I did, I would not lose many patients any more. I'm glad you came so I could see for myself that Diamondola is still alive. I believe this is what can be called a miracle. I wish I possessed this healing power."

## CHAPTER XXX
## *The Trip of the Yellow Satchel*

*"Know ye not that the unrighteous shall not inherit the kingdom of God? Be not deceived: neither ... thieves, nor covetous, ... shall inherit the kingdom of God" (1 Cor. 6: 9, 10).*

Why was Diamondola not resurrected to complete health and strength immediately? She understood it all very clearly now. The pain she suffered during the months it took her bedsores to heal was as nothing in comparison with the joy she felt as she watched Miss Vosilika's baptism. A short time later Diamondola experienced further joy when she attended Miss Vosilika's marriage to a good Adventist young man by the name of Loizo. And a few months later her cup overflowed when she attended the baptism of Mrs. Loizo's older sister and her two daughters. Yes, those few months of suffering were worth the four souls who were brought into the kingdom of God as a result of those nightly Bible studies when pain kept the patient from sleeping. Those four people were instrumental in influencing others to join the ranks of the church too. Diamondola could see now that even during sickness and suffering God had helped her improve those moments to His glory and had turned evil into good. The members of this family not only became members of the church for life but have ever remained fast friends of Diamondola.

Both Elder Erzberger and Diamondola, now well recovered from their illnesses, were able to take up their work with renewed energy. They took an inventory of the mission situation. The office, church, and living facilities in the city, which the mission was renting, were far from ideal. The refugees spilled into the office space and church, and made any semblance of order and efficiency impossible. It was imperative that a place be found in which the growing family of widows, orphans, and office workers could live. The children needed a place for recreation, and the adults needed a place to relax from the tensions brought on by the war and their recent illnesses. A large home on the outskirts of the city was rented by the mission for these purposes.

The office staff and those who were staying at the mission moved out to Rumeli Hissar during the early months of 1920. The children were thrilled with the large garden and spent many hours playing out of doors in spite of the cold and snow. Mrs. Erzberger and Mrs. Keanides spent many happy hours renovating the nine-bedroom house, tending the children, and running the place as a communal home. One large room next to the kitchen was used as the dining room. The large center room was furnished with an organ and living room furnishings. This was the parlor and it was also used for morning and evening worship. There was a large playroom and a play area in the garden assigned to the children. Then each family unit was given one of the nine bedrooms. The extra bedrooms were reserved for guests and possible additions. The office and church were still situated in the original rented building in the city, because of its central location.

That spring of 1920, after an absence of thirteen years, Alexandra was able to return to Turkey for a visit. With her came Ares' invalid mother, who was suffering from tuberculosis. All Mrs. Aresian's relatives had been killed in the Iconium massacres and deportations, so she was welcomed into the Adventist communal home in Rumeli Hissar.

Mrs. Keanides thoroughly enjoyed Alexandra's visit. The two of them even made a trip to Brousa, and had the pleasure of visiting old friends and neighbors.

Mr. and Mrs. O. Bezirdjian arrived from Egypt and joined the force of workers in Turkey. They moved into the Rumeli Hissar house that year, and Mr. Bezirdjian took up the ministerial work in Constantinople. This relieved Elder Tcharakian so that he could go to Iconium to reconstruct and re-establish the work there.

In May, Aram Ashod arrived from Egypt. Since he also was a linguist and translator and had had training in business and office work, Elder Erzberger invited him to join the office staff. The office was swamped with requests for literature from distant parts of Turkey where an isolated member here or there had summoned the courage to return to his old home. Correspondence was piling up and the office was far behind in its schedule, owing to the months of sickness of Erzberger and Diamondola, but under the new arrangement the office began to return to normal.

Diamondola and Mrs. Keanides were sorry when it was time for Alexandra to return to her work in Greece. But they hoped that since the world situation seemed settled, there would be no more such long separations. Ares' mother stayed on at Rumeli Hissar. Theodora was determined to be her special nurse.

Reports from isolated members became encouraging again as a few members assembled in various places and spread the truth the best they could without ministerial assistance. In Iconium, Tcharakian was meeting with success. The two other surviving ministers traveled about the field visiting the churches, and sent in encouraging reports. The force of workers was depleted compared with the prewar years, but everyone felt that in some way God would send more workers to join the ranks.

That summer of 1920 the Adventists in Constantinople were favored by a visit from Guy Dail, an American who was secretary of the Central European Division. He was pleased with the farsightedness of the office staff in moving out to Rumeli Hissar, and was happily surprised to see the nineteen members of the household working together so harmoniously.

One morning Elder Dail, the Erzbergers, Ashod, and Diamondola went down to the office in Galata. Diamondola was sent to the bank to draw out two hundred Turkish lira with which to pay bills and purchase equipment for the office, which Elder Dail felt they should no longer do without. Two hundred Turkish lira was a lot of money in those days. It was sufficient to pay the workers' monthly salaries, pay for some printing and office bills, and buy the extra supplies Elder Dail had recommended. As Diamondola packed the lira into her new yellow satchel, she felt she was being watched, but she shrugged off her suspicions, tucked her yellow satchel bulging with bills under her arm, and walked hurriedly from the bank to the office.

Diamondola entered the mission building and closed the door behind her. She placed the yellow satchel on her desk, but before she had time to put the money in the safe the doorbell rang. The door was opened and a suspicious-looking stranger was admitted.

Elder Dail glanced at the man and asked, "What does this man want?"

Diamondola repeated the question to the stranger in Turkish. He quickly replied, "I want money. I'm a poor Greek refugee from Iconium. I am a teacher, but the Kemalistic movement group chased me and my family out of our home. My wife and children are sick and hungry and are living in a little hut near here. Please give me some money to buy them some food."

"What church do you belong to? Each denomination is caring for the needs of its refugees," Diamondola informed the man.

"I don't have a special church, so I came to you," he replied.

"Let's give him a lira or two and get rid of him," suggested Diamondola.

"No, no!" disagreed Elder Dail, then suggested, "Diamondola and Mrs. Erzberger, you two go with the man and investigate his case. If he really needs money, we will help him. If not, he shouldn't receive any money."

The three experienced workers in Turkey opposed this suggestion, for they knew the ways of the country and how dangerous thieves sometimes disguised themselves as beggars, but in deference to the visiting minister they said little. To them it seemed unwise to send two women with a strange man across town to investigate his needs. Constantinople was swarming with thieves and murderers at this time. But no one wanted to offend the division guest, and so only mild opposition was offered to his plan.

Consequently Mrs. Erzberger and Diamondola started to leave on their assignment. Shortly before she left the office, Diamondola's cousin, Rumatica, who worked as a governess in a wealthy Greek home in the city, entered the office and was planning to spend her day off with Diamondola. As Diamondola left the office she looked apologetically at Rumatica, who understood, and urged Diamondola to hurry and complete her errand. Rumatica assured Diamondola that she would knit or read while she was gone.

"Oh, Rumatica, you're an understanding dear," Diamondola called from the doorway in Greek. "It will be a while before I get back because

Mrs. Erzberger wants me to help her do a bit of shopping for our orphan children before I return. I should be back shortly after lunch. I'll see you then. 'Bye." With that the women left the office with the strange man.

Two blocks from the office the man asked them to please give him a Turkish lira so that he could buy some bread to take home with them. They gladly gave him the lira and waited outside the shop while the man went inside to make the purchase. But he didn't return. Time passed, and finally they recognized that the man had been gone quite a while. Diamondola stuck her head in under the awning of the open shop and looked around.

Not seeing the man, she asked the shop owner, "What happened to the man who came into your shop a little bit ago?"

"Oh, he just took one look at you and ran out the other side," he answered.

"Well, what do you know?" exclaimed Mrs. Erzberger with relief, "we got rid of our beggar for one Turkish lira after all. And what is more, we can run right downtown now and do our shopping. We'll get through sooner than I had expected. Maybe your mother and I can even start sewing today on the shirts and dresses for the children."

"Yes, and I can get back to the office, visit my cousin, and get some work done before closing time," added Diamondola.

After Diamondola returned to her office, the young office girl who assisted her asked, "Why did you send that man back after your yellow satchel?"

"What do you mean?" asked Diamondola absent-mindedly.

"Shortly after you left here this morning with that poor man, he returned and said, 'Miss Diamondola is at our place and she asks that you send Rumatica with me with the yellow satchel that she left on her desk.' So Rumatica took the yellow satchel and left with the man. I thought she'd come back with you. Her things are all here ..."

"Alice," interrupted Diamondola tensely, suddenly grasping the significance of what the girl was saying, "you haven't given my yellow satchel full of mission money to that thief, have you?"

"Oh, no!" moaned Alice, sliding down onto her chair as the truth dawned on her. "Honestly, Diamondola, I didn't know it had money in it—neither did Rumatica. And to think the poor girl went with that rascal ..."

"Oh, dear," cried Diamondola. "I know it's not your fault, Alice, but someone had better know where my cousin is———." With that she sped into Elder Erzberger's office, where he and Elder Dail were in conference. "Where is my Rumatica?" she demanded in agitation.

"Why, I really don't know, Diamondola. Shortly after you left this morning, Brother Dail and I went out to look at the new property we hope to purchase. She was with Alice when we left, I'm sure. Is something wrong? Can't you find her?" questioned Elder Erzberger gravely as he noted the look of distress on Diamondola's blanched face.

"No, I can't find Rumatica, nor the yellow satchel full of mission money. What is more, Rumatica went with that—that—beggar more than four hours ago. She's probably in great danger, if he hasn't already———." Diamondola sank into a chair and covered her face with her hands.

Their only hope lay in trusting God to exercise control over the wicked man and give protection to the innocent girl. So they prayed.

Toward evening a bedraggled Rumatica rang the office bell, and a relieved office force welcomed the girl back. Together the group reconstructed the story that had led up to theft of the yellow satchel. The clever thief evidently had listened carefully to the office conversation during the few minutes he was in the office. He had remembered Diamondola's mentioning Rumatica's name, and this was the reason he had mentioned her by name as the one who was to accompany him with the yellow satchel to Diamondola. Apparently, he had observed Diamondola in the bank, and knew the satchel contained money. When the cunning thief got Rumatica out on the streets, he led her into a deserted blind alley.

"Give me that yellow satchel," he had whispered threateningly to her, "and don't yell for help or I'll knife you!"

Rumatica, guessing that the satchel contained money, refused to give it to the thief. She tried to run away, but the thief grabbed her roughly and shoved her against the wall, then wrenched the satchel from her grasp and sped away down the street. Rumatica, frightened beyond words, fainted and collapsed on the road. Soon she regained consciousness. She looked around. The scoundrel was gone, and so was the yellow satchel. Rumatica ran frantically from street to street trying to find her way in this strange section of town. At first she hardly dared inquire for help, but as the sun sank lower in the west, she began to ask from shop to shop until she got into familiar territory and found her way back to the office.

The office would have to get along without the two hundred lira, and Diamondola would have to get along without the new yellow satchel, but they were all thankful that Rumatica had survived a dangerous experience.

*Diamondola's wedding picture.*

## CHAPTER XXXI
# To Love and to Cherish

*"There be three things which are too wonderful for me, yea, four which I know not: the way of an eagle in the air; the way of a serpent upon a rock; the way of a ship in the midst of the sea; and the way of a man with a maid"*
*(Prov. 30:18, 19).*

While Brother Dail was still visiting in the Turkish Mission it was decided that if the division voted their approval, an orphanage and school would be started in Constantinople. The Erzbergers were voted a furlough. Before Diamondola was to be separated from the Erzbergers, she and they were invited to make a trip to Zurich, Switzerland, to attend the first large European general conference to be held in twelve years.

Diamondola was so excited that she could hardly collect her wits enough to plan for her trip to Europe. But Mother, calm and collected, chose just the right outfits for Diamondola's European tour. Aram Ashod helped her, too. Diamondola wanted a black velvet dress that would be appropriate for dress wear in Europe. Diamondola had always been a poor shopper, but Aram was shrewd in business and knew quality materials. He agreed to make the selection for her. Secretly he was happy to do so, for he was eager to become more important and necessary to Diamondola.

When Aram brought home the package of fine, soft velvet, Diamondola was truly grateful and expressed her appreciation.

"You are very welcome, Little Diamond," he assured her. "I will always be happy to be at your service." Then he smiled and looked straight into her eyes. "Don't you know that for three years I have thought of you? All the while I was in prison camp I was thinking of you. I, well, I was hoping that you had not married while I was away. I have been back only a few weeks, and in this busy, train-station household, I have had very few moments alone with you. Now you are going away. But just remember that someone will be thinking of you in a special way."

"Oh, Aram," Diamondola said blushing. "You mustn't say such things. I'm like your sister. You've just been paying too much attention to the children's little ditties—'Aram likes Diamondola, Diamondola likes Aram.' I've heard them, too. I want you to know that I have not put these ideas into their heads. Children have strange ideas and like to have a bit of fun."

"Diamondola, don't try to dodge the issue," he responded. "You are twenty-six and I am ten years older than you. We are not too young to think and plan for a future together, are we?"

"Please, Aram," Diamondola said, moving away. "I cannot think clearly just now. My mind is in such a whirl over this European conference—I must have time to think. Please don't rush me. I have always thought of you as a brother. I'll have to have time to think."

He folded his arms and stepped directly in front of her, then smiled at her and said, "All right, Diamondola, I won't rush you. Just don't get lost in Europe, or I'll be tempted to go there and look you up. Will you write to me?"

"Of course I will," she readily agreed. "And, Aram, will you make an agreement with me?"

"I am willing to make several agreements with you, my dear," he teased. "I don't suppose we have the same plan in mind at this moment, do we?"

"Oh, let's get off the subject, Aram," she chided, a bit embarrassed by his persistence. "My mother is largely an unlettered woman. I will send all my letters to her. Will you read them to her for me? And then if there is an 'A' on the outside of the envelope, you'll know that there is a special enclosure to you."

"Must I read the enclosure to her as well?" he smiled.

"Stop teasing now, but you may if you wish. You may be sure the letters won't be that personal," said Diamondola emphatically as she whisked out of the room and hurried upstairs to her own room with the velvet material draped over her arm.

Upstairs she found her mother in the room of Ares' mother. She showed the ladies the fine piece of velvet Aram had purchased for her.

"Ah, my daughter," sighed Mrs. Aresian, "Ares is gone; but I wish above all things that I could see you married to a fine young Adventist worker before my death. I like that young bachelor downstairs. Aram Ashod is a fine man and would be my choice for you, my dear, if you could find it in your heart to love him. He is not only wise and a good Christian, but see how kind he is. He chose such a lovely piece of material for you." Ares' mother rubbed the material between her fingers to feel its fine texture.

*Oh, dear,* sighed Diamondola to herself, *what's wrong with everyone tonight? Why can't I be left alone?* Diamondola's mind was occupied with other things. But not wanting to offend anyone, she answered tactfully, "Aram is indeed a fine man. He is like my brother. Maybe in time, Mother Aresian, I will agree to a marriage arrangement, but right now I am busy with my plans to go to Europe."

"You are right, my daughter," agreed the sick woman, "but I do not approve of your remaining single. Ares would not either. He would want you to marry. And I could readily ask God's blessing on your marriage with Aram Ashod."

"Thank you for thinking of me, Mother Aresian," said Diamondola with sincere appreciation, "and I will see how God leads me."

The next day as the sun was coming up Diamondola rose early to stroll alone in the rose garden. She was so excited she had hardly slept. Was it her trip to Europe, or was it thoughts of Aram Ashod that had kept her awake all night? She didn't know. Perhaps it was both, she thought, as she plucked a yellow rose.

Diamondola was not aware that Aram and Mrs. Aresian were watching her. They had also risen early and were sitting quietly upstairs on the veranda. As Diamondola crossed the garden path into the summer sunshine on the far side of the garden, Mrs. Aresian spoke her thoughts plainly to the young man beside her.

"Aram," she said, looking at Diamondola, "there is a lovely maiden. Diamondola is a real jewel—as perfect as the yellow rose in her hand. I wish, my son, that you would make her your wife. I could rest in peace if

I knew that her wound for the love of my son was healed by the love of a man as worthy as you. I wish that you would marry her. She is so intelligent, so capable—but she needs manly protection and love. I hope that you can fulfill my desire for her."

"I hope I can too," admitted Aram candidly, then added, "Thank you for your confidence in me. Maybe someday Diamondola can learn to love me; and if she does, I know that I can love her. Diamondola's hurt has been a long time in healing. But maybe, if I am patient, I shall win her heart. Thank you again," he said as he walked into the house.

It was midsummer when good-byes were said and the Erzbergers and Diamondola were off by boat and train to Europe. The three stopped first in Salonika. What fun it was for the three sisters—Diamondola, Alexandra, and Susanna—to be together again. Susanna's oldest son had emigrated to the United States, and her youngest son was talking of going to America, too. Diamondola didn't blame them. That was certainly the safest place to be, it seemed; but her place was wherever God called her to work.

And Turkey seemed to be the place He had designated for her, so she said facetiously, never dreaming that someday her words would be fulfilled, "I'll go to the States and see you all; Susanna and her family, Despina and her family, and, well, are you going too, Alexandra?"

Alexandra was not so sure. She might go there to retire, she thought, if she lived through her active years of mission service. Diamondola agreed that that was the way things stood for her too. Maybe someday the family would all retire together in America—but not yet.

While she was in Salonika, Diamondola persuaded Susanna and her youngest son to go to Constantinople and stay with Mother during her absence.

"And by the way," she added, "please keep an eye on Aram Ashod and give me your opinion."

From Salonika the three went to Athens, then sailed to Italy. In Naples and Rome they visited all the interesting sights. Finally they reached Switzerland.

During August, 1920, the European conference met, and Diamondola was privileged to hear and see such leaders of the Adventist denomination as A. G. Daniells, W. A. Spicer, L. H. Christian, and others. The spiritual refreshment the conference members received was stimulating, and the plans that were laid were steppingstones to greater victories for the

Lord's cause. The conference voted to establish an orphanage in Turkey for the Levant Union. The Erzbergers and Diamondola were also voted a few months' vacation in Europe. The brethren felt that these workers deserved a rest to try to recover from the effects of their recent illnesses and the war.

At the meetings Diamondola was called upon to tell some of her experiences during the war.

The workers left the conference determined to achieve greater exploits for God. During the two-month leave of absence in Europe, Diamondola stayed for a time at Skodsburg Sanitarium in Denmark. She visited the Voights and Bridde in Germany. Diamondola encouraged Mrs. Voight to remain in the church, and she still greatly admired Carl Voight for his honest ways. Although he was no longer a member of the church and had lost faith in the Scriptures, he never tried to persuade his wife or anyone else to follow his personal beliefs. He never worked against the church to Diamondola's knowledge, and ever remained a true friend of his former church and friends.

Before Diamondola left Europe, Elder Christian assured her that the Erzbergers would return to the Levant Union. Then, after her leave of absence, Diamondola hurried back to Constantinople and her work. She was welcomed by all the members of the Rumeli Hissar Advent household, especially by Aram and her mother. But she noticed that Ares' mother was missing. It was then she learned that Mrs. Aresian had passed away as a result of tuberculosis late that summer.

The mission work soon swept Diamondola back into her former busy routine. The first thing after the household worship each morning, she was off to the office with Aram and Elder Greaves, who was substituting for Elder Erzberger while the latter finished his furlough. At noon they had lunch together in the office, and then late in the evening they would return home together. In order to enjoy each other's company alone, and at the same time get a little extra fresh air, Diamondola and Aram would walk each evening to a neighbor who sold milk to the household. Aram insisted that Diamondola drink a full cup to refresh her before they reached the house. He thought this would help her keep her cheeks as pink as they had been when she came from Europe.

One day Diamondola bought some luscious-looking strawberries and sent Aram a heaping bowlful carefully arranged, and bearing a little note that read, "Just for you, Aram, from Diamondola."

Gradually they seemed to be drawing toward each other, but there were ups and downs ahead in their romance.

One evening as they were walking home carrying the pails of milk, Aram stopped, set down his pail, and asked, "Diamondola, when are we going to get married?"

"Oh, I don't know," she said casually, walking on with her pail of milk. "We'll have to think about it," she added without even turning her head or slowing her pace.

This reaction was frustrating to Aram. Pursing his lips, he drew a deep breath, exhaled explosively and hastened his steps to keep stride with her. In his rush some of the milk sloshed over the bucket, spattering his polished black shoes. Had Aram been able to read her mind, he would have seen that Diamondola's thoughts belied her actions. But he couldn't, and he felt frustrated. He wondered what to say next. Watching her intently out of the corner of his eye, he stumbled along, and finally tried again. "When will you know, Diamondola?"

"Oh, after we've prayed about it," she responded as casually as ever, never even glancing his way.

When they finally reached the gate Aram set his pail down with another splash. Blocking Diamondola's passage, he said earnestly, "Look, Diamondola, everyone expects us to be married. We know each other well, and we are in love, aren't we? Why wait?" Without moving an inch, Diamondola placed her pail deliberately between them, and looked into Aram's eyes. "Aram," she said, "do you mind if we pray about it a little more?"

"As you say, Diamondola," he agreed.

Aram had taken over most of the actual publishing work for the union. He also helped Diamondola with more and more of the accounts. On some days when Diamondola had only translation work to do, she stayed at home and did this work in her room.

It was on one of these days that Diamondola had an experience that changed the course of her life. Early one afternoon she was home translating, when she suddenly had an overpowering urge to walk over to the window and look out. She repressed the impulse several times, but finally yielded and walked over to the window. As she looked up the path leading from the boat landing she saw Aram coming up the path. She smiled and waved to him, and Aram returned the greeting.

Diamondola instinctively knew that what had just happened had special significance. A few moments later Aram burst into the room. Walking confidently over to Diamondola, and taking her in his arms, he kissed her and said, "Don't refuse any longer. I have prayed about the matter and my prayer was answered—you were standing in the window."

"I will, Aram, I will," Diamondola answered submissively.

The next Sabbath, Aram and Diamondola's engagement was announced in the church and all were invited to attend the engagement party on the lawn at Rumeli Hissar the following Sunday.

The next eleven months passed quickly. Diamondola and Aram worked together in the office, and planned for their wedding. Weddings were simple affairs in those days. The bride-to-be was given a few choice pieces of material by the groom to prepare her trousseau. Aram bought the finest materials that his mission salary would allow, and on the way home from work they often stopped at the dressmaker's house so that Diamondola would get a dress that fitted perfectly. Mother Keanides embroidered some pillow slips, sheets, and table scarfs for the couple. Other friends contributed other gifts. Diamondola and Aram decided to wait until the Erzbergers returned to Constantinople before they got married so Elder Erzberger could perform the ceremony. The wedding took place on September 21, 1921. All the Adventists in the area attended the marriage ceremony of their favorite worker. Diamondola had endeared herself to the hearts of all in the Turkish mission and they were glad to see her happily married to a capable worker in the cause of God.

Together the Ashods continued their labor for God until 1963 when he officially retired from active service. In September, 1963, the Ashods flew to California, where they were briefly re-united with the other three Keanides sisters—Alexandra, Susanna, and Despina. Friends in the Middle East will always remember the contributions of Diamondola to the early Advent work in those lands, and to her is this text particularly applicable:

"A book of remembrance was written before him for them that feared the LORD, and that thought upon his name. And they shall be mine, saith the LORD of hosts, in that day when I make up my jewels" (Mal. 3:16, 17). Surely Diamondola's name is written in that book of remembrance for she is one of those jewels. Those who have been inspired by her life and work are convinced that although her name means "little Diamond," in heaven she will be one of the shining stars.

We invite you to view the complete
selection of titles we publish at:

www.TEACHServices.com

scan with your mobile
device to go directly
to our website

Please write or email us your praises, reactions, or
thoughts about this or any other book we publish at:

11 Quartermaster Circle
Fort Oglethorpe, GA 30742

**Info@TEACHServices.com**

TEACH Services, Inc., titles may be purchased in bulk for
educational, business, fund-raising, or sales promotional use.
For information, please e-mail:

**BulkSales@TEACHServices.com**

Finally if you are interested in seeing
your own book in print, please contact us at

**publishing@TEACHServices.com**

We would be happy to review your manuscript for free.

www.ingramcontent.com/pod-product-compliance
Lightning Source LLC
Chambersburg PA
CBHW070538170426
43200CB00011B/2462